Haifa Republic

Haifa Republic
A Democratic Future
for Israel

OMRI BOEHM

nyrb **New York Review Books** New York

This is a New York Review Book

published by The New York Review of Books

435 Hudson Street, New York, NY 10014

www.nyrb.com

LIBRARY OF CONGRESS CATALOGING-IN-PUBLICATION DATA
Names: Boehm, Omri, author.
Title: Haifa Republic: a democratic future for Israel / Omri Boehm.
Description: New York City: New York Review Books, 2020. | Series:
    New York Review Books
Identifiers: LCCN 2019039530 (print) | LCCN 2019039531 (ebook) |
    ISBN 9781681373935 (paperback) | ISBN 9781681373942 (ebook)
Subjects: LCSH: Zionism. | Arab-Israeli conflict. | Israel—Ethnic
    relations. | Israel—Politics and government.
Classification: LCC DS149 .B63 2020 (print) | LCC DS149 (ebook) |
    DDC 320.95694—dc23
LC record available at https://lccn.loc.gov/2019039530
LC ebook record available at https://lccn.loc.gov/2019039531

ISBN 978-1-68137-393-5
Available as an electronic book; ISBN 978-1-68137-394-2

Printed in the United States of America on acid-free paper.

1 2 3 4 5 6 7 8 9 10

For Inbal

If you will it, it is no dream.

—Theodor Herzl

Contents

Introduction

1.

IN THE TWENTY-FIVE YEARS THAT have passed since the assassination of Yitzhak Rabin, his two-state Oslo legacy has been driven into the ground. In 1993, when the agreement was first signed, approximately 110,000 settlers were living in the West Bank, and 146,000 were living in occupied territories surrounding Jerusalem. By now, the numbers have increased to approximately 400,000 settlers in the West Bank and 300,000 around Jerusalem.[1] This situation will not be reversed. In 2021, roughly 10 percent of Israel's Jewish population lives on occupied territory—subject to Israeli law, represented by Israel's parliament—and enjoys the opportunities and prosperity of a flourishing first-world country, with public schools, factories, banks, a system of highways, and a research university at their disposal. Around them, however, are almost 3 million Palestinians who, for 53 years now, have lived under Israel's aggressive military regime.

Even intransigent two-state supporters agree that not all of these settlers can be evacuated, but they insist that the challenge posed by their presence is exaggerated. On this view, whereas the West Bank's map is stained by approximately 130 spots marking Israeli settlements, about 110 of them count populations of less than 5,000. Another 60 settlements, the argument goes, have populations of less than 1,000, and many of them are, in the first place, located next to the 1967 border: by introducing only minor corrections to the border, it is allegedly possible to leave most settlers within Israel's proper territory, and to compensate the Palestinians with other pieces of land from other areas. Given this, it is claimed that the tendency to "grossly overstate" the obstacle that settlements pose to a future two-state solution is based not on a sober analysis of the situation, but on an ideological support of one-state politics.[2]

Unfortunately, this optimism is itself highly ideological, and can only be preserved if one avoids a careful look at the map. Surprisingly to many, the main obstacle has nothing to do with the number of settlers, but with the number of Palestinians. In the territory between the Jordan River and the Mediterranean Sea currently lives a Palestinian majority, constituting approximately 53 percent of the population. Yet even the most "generous" two-state programs offer this population about 22 percent of the land. We have grown accustomed to ignore this fact, and to see this arrangement as a reasonable, desired compromise. The truth is that it isn't, and not merely because it is unjust: offering sovereignty to the majority of the population on this tiny and discontinuous fraction of the territory isn't the type of compromise that can bring peace.

And then again the number of settlers must also be considered. While it is true that about 110 West Bank settlements have less than 5,000 inhabitants, this leaves 20 settlements counting more than 5,000, and some of them counting significantly more. Modi'in Illit, a settlement not far from Jerusalem, counts more than 70,000 inhabitants; Beitar Illit, 55,000; Ma'ale Adumim, 40,000; and the list goes on. To understand the significance of these figures, consider Israel's evacuation of settlers from the Gaza Strip, in 2005. In total, 8,400 settlers were removed from a land that is not nearly as sacred to Jews or symbolic to Israelis as the West Bank, and the event is still remembered as traumatic to Israeli society. Also, the idea that most settlements are located along the '67 border is misleading. Whereas the largest settlements indeed are located near the border, numerous others are located *very* deep in the territory. Ariel, one of Israel's most prosperous settlements—population 20,000—is positioned at the heart of the West Bank. Its location was strategically chosen in the 1970s to interrupt any possible geographical continuity of a future Palestinian state. Speaking in 1980 as Israel's minister of

defense, Ariel Sharon had already referred to the settlement project as a fait accompli, a "skeleton" that had been laid down in the
West Bank and would prevent any territorial compromise. Given
this "skeleton," he said, "I don't see now any area that can be
handed [over] to anybody."[3] When he spoke, a settlement like
Ariel counted only a few hundred inhabitants. In 2018, Sheldon
Adelson, the casino mogul who served as Trump's chief donor,
contributed the necessary sum for the founding of Ariel University's Adelson School of Medicine. Sharon's "skeleton" is now a
fully formed, heavy body. At some point one must admit that
the two-state dream has faded into a two-state illusion. Ignoring
this fact is akin to denying global warming.

Meanwhile, the idea of an enlarged Jewish state encompassing
the West Bank is gaining currency, both in Israel and interna-
tionally. Almost immediately after he had assumed office, President Trump signaled that he would back out of the two-state
commitment to which US presidents—Democrats and Repub-
licans alike—had remained loyal for decades. When Trump's
so-called Deal of the Century emerged, Israelis across the political
spectrum started explicitly advocating annexations as well.
During Obama's presidency, even Netanyahu paid occasional lip
service to the two-state solution, proclaiming a "vision of peace"
in which the two peoples would live "freely side-by-side," each
with "its own flag, its own national anthem, its own govern-

ment."[4] The Obama administration countenanced this open lie because it helped mitigate escalating feuds with Israel's government and spared the president a clash with America's Jewish community. The mainstream liberal media was getting comfortable with Netanyahu's lies as well. Whether we like it or not, Trump's presidency shattered the hypocrisy: the position of the Israeli government has hardly changed in practice, but it now speaks truthfully of what it has been doing all along, namely preventing a Palestinian state and promoting annexations. Significantly, this is not just a Netanyahu policy; his party, Likud, embraced annexation officially in 2017. Blue and White, as well as Yesh Atid, Israel's "center-left" opposition, have also been enthusiastic about the Deal of the Century—and no longer even pay lip service to the idea of a Palestinian state. If a Biden-Harris administration wishes to backpedal to the old familiar politics, it will be sure to fail: there is no going back to the two-state lie, let alone to the two-state solution. A new generation of Democrats refusing to accept ethnic nationalism obviously knows this well. Yet what is there for liberal democrats in Israel or the US to offer in place of the defunct two-state solution? What is the plan?

Israel's Basic Laws, which stand in for the country's constitution, are currently being rapidly revised in ways that reinforce the same trend and raise the same unsettling questions. Though Israel's 1948 Declaration of Independence asserts somewhat generally that Jews have the "right for self-determination" in Eretz Israel—thus accommodating the possibility, at least, of Palestinian self-determination—Israel's 2018 nation-state law specifies that this right is "unique to the Jewish people." Preparing the legal infrastructure for massive annexations—anticipating the moment at which "too many" Arabs will live within Israel's declared borders—the law also revokes the status of Arabic as an official language in Israel, and defines "Jewish settlement" of Eretz Israel as a "national value," thus undermining the declaration's pledge to equality, irrespective of "religion or race." The nation-state law constitutes a dramatic step towards establishing a one-Jewish-state "solution."

In recent years, right-wing legislators such as Naftali Bennett, Moshe Ya'alon, Ayelet Shaked, and others have begun to promote political plans that could be called "apartheid with a human face," plans now effectively accepted by Likud's central committee. The idea is to annex large portions of the West Bank and stop subjecting Palestinians to Israel's military regime—but without granting them a sovereign state or full citizenship. The model for such a "humane apartheid" is the status quo in Jerusalem. Unlike the rest of the West Bank, the city's eastern parts were annexed by Israel immediately after the Six-Day War, with its Arab inhabitants becoming permanent residents of Israel, but not citizens. (Unlike Arab Israeli citizens, they cannot vote for the Knesset.)

The general public, as well as government officials, journalists, lawmakers, police officers, and judges—and also the international community—have come to accept this as entirely normal, and it provides a convenient model for the future in other areas of the West Bank.

Less moderate voices support not just apartheid but transfer, or ethnic cleansing—an idea that is being rehabilitated at the heart of Israeli politics. Amiram Levin, a former top Israel Defense Forces major general publicly perceived as a liberal Zionist, suggested in 2017 that in the next round of hostilities, Israel should "tear the Palestinians apart," to make sure that "they do not stay." He proposed "kick[ing] them to the other side of the Jordan River."[5] In 2019, Bezalel Smotrich, leader of the religious Zionist party Tkuma, said to *Israel Hayom*, Israel's largest daily: "As far as I'm concerned, let Gaza rot, let them die of hunger, of thirst and of malaria." This policy, he says, should be accompanied by opening "Gaza's gates to massive emigration," otherwise known in Israel as "voluntary transfer."[6] Smotrich may be the leader of an extreme-right religious Zionist party, but as he drafted this plan, in 2019, he was also a minister and a member of cabinet. For that matter, Trump's so-called Deal of the Century also raised the possibility of population swaps and the denaturalization of Arab Israeli citizens in what is sometimes called the Triangle Area—a region that is heavily populated with Arab

Israelis and borders the West Bank. As Israel's former defense minister, Avigdor Lieberman, tweeted immediately after the announcement of the plan: "In 2004, when I suggested a plan for population swaps, everybody raised an eyebrow. But just now President Trump adopted the full plan ... Standing by your principles and being patient pays off." In 2014, when he was Israel's foreign minister, Lieberman ran on a platform calling for the transfer of Arab Israelis from Acre, Haifa, and Jaffa to the West Bank and neighboring Arab countries. Lieberman was once considered an outlier, an extremist; today, he is seen as a pragmatist, a moderate, and indeed a pillar of what passes for Israel's center-left.

We should listen very carefully to these calls for ethnic cleansing. Israelis have always wavered between repressing and boasting about the fact that, in 1948, a Jewish democracy with a Jewish majority was enabled through massive expulsions of Palestinians. Seventy-three years later, with no prospect of two separate states and the Palestinians soon again to become the majority of Israel's population, Israelis still shun any responsibility for these crimes. Political despair, in combination with a violent ethnic conflict, threatens a catastrophe. If we continue to ignore reality and to refuse to imagine an alternative we can fight for, the result will be much worse than apartheid. Israel's right wing has its solutions—annexation, apartheid, expulsion—while liberal democrats have failed to come up with any. This is true not just of Israel's now nonexistent parties of the left, but also of organizations like B'Tselem, Peace Now, J Street, or the New Israel Fund. They are united against the occupation—B'Tselem just now took the step of explicitly labeling it apartheid—but can they make any meaningful political progress without having a viable goal they can fight *for*?

The reason for the inability to offer an alternative positive agenda is not difficult to find. Committed as these liberals are to the principle of a Jewish democracy, they require separation from the Palestinians in order to ensure a Jewish majority. And though separation is now plainly untenable, democratic visions for Israel beyond the two-state solution are perceived as anti-Zionist forms of betrayal—quite literally, as treason. Accordingly, liberal Zionists can only seek refuge in criticizing Netanyahu's corruption, fighting for the legalization of light drugs, and promoting women's and gay rights: important objectives, but also ways *not* to talk about Gaza, the occupation of the West Bank, and the future of a country where liberal democracy is ever more at risk.

As these monumental transformations beyond two-state politics take shape, leading left-leaning Israelis and liberal Zionist voices (think David Grossman, Amos Oz, Ari Shavit, Avishai Margalit, or Michael Walzer, among many others) are lagging dangerously behind. Clinging to the lost hope for a Jewish liberal democracy—and, yes, for a sustainable ethnic Jewish majority—they continue backing separation plans that have been losing credibility since the late 1990s. What once was an audacious rational perspective on Israeli politics has stagnated into an irresponsible bad faith. It is long past time for liberal Zionist thinkers to think again.

Consider Amos Oz's *Dear Zealots*, his last political statement, in which Oz reaffirmed his longstanding support for two-state politics while dismissing leftists seeking one-state alternatives as, at best, a "sad joke," or, worse, as dangerous moral fanatics.[7] Oz knew particularly well that the situation had dramatically changed in the course of fifty years, but he remained unimpressed by what Israelis call "the facts on the ground." In his view, the facts only served as excuses for fanatics: the "extreme right" and the "anti-Zionist" left had, as he saw it, entered a "secret pact, a conspiracy," brainwashing us with the idea that the occupation is "irreversible." "Irreversible," Oz wrote, was the word that "irritated" him, that "outraged" him. His idea, which some falsely acclaimed as prophetic, was basically that it is always possible to use the imagination in order to conceive a return to the past.[8]

Oz's praise of the imagination as a counterweight to the idea of "irreversibility" was in fact a reactionary obfuscation. Gramsci famously stated that times of political "crisis" are times when "the old is dying, and the new cannot yet be born."[9] At these times,

Gramsci predicts, intellectuals belonging to the cultural hegemony will seek to anchor people's nostalgia to the dying ideologies of the past, thus aggravating the crisis. In Israel, which has been trapped in a Gramscian crisis for a long time now, the old political slogans—"Jewish and democratic," "liberal Zionism," "the two-state solution"—are rapidly becoming empty clichés. By continuing to ignore the facts on the ground, by continuing to insist on the two-state solution, by refusing to rethink the relation between Israel and Zionism, liberal intellectuals have allowed the conversation about the country's future to decline into a shouting match between chauvinistic Zionism on the right and anti-Israeli critique on the anti-Zionist left.

Haifa Republic argues, by contrast, that the vital center can still be reclaimed, articulating an alternative to two-state politics from within a liberal Zionist perspective. True Israeli patriots must now challenge Zionist taboos as we have come to know them, must dare to imagine the country's transformation, from a Jewish state into a federal, binational republic. Contrary to common misconceptions, passionately held by Zionists and anti-Zionists alike, such a transformation is neither post- nor anti-Zionist. It represents a type of politics that was a matter of consensus for many long years among Zionism's founding fathers: for the greater part of their careers, Theodor Herzl, Vladimir (Ze'ev) Jabotinsky, Ahad Ha'am, and David Ben-Gurion could all agree on it. Future leaders—on the left and the right—can and ought to agree on such politics as well. Rehabilitating Zionism's binational origins is the only alternative to apartheid and expulsions and the only way to sustain liberal Zionist aspirations in the twenty-first century: securing a democratic homeland in which Jewish citizens exercise national self-determination—alongside Palestinian compatriots doing the same—in a joint, sovereign state.

2.

For years, one-state politics has been condemned as anti-Zionist, not to say anti-Semitic. Many will remember the cold reception given to Tony Judt's 2003 essay "Israel: The Alternative," which announced the two-state solution's de facto collapse, and the need to transform Israel from Jewish ethnostate to a single binational republic. Things had changed since Oslo, Judt wrote, and in a world where nation-states were becoming passé the idea of Israel as a Jewish state was rapidly becoming a dysfunctional "anachronism." Future liberal democrats would not accept the idea that, in Israel, "one community—Jews—is set above others."[10]

The article was mocked and denounced. Leon Wieseltier set the tone in *The New Republic*, arguing that Judt and his editors at *The New York Review of Books* "crossed the line" from legitimate criticism of Israel's "policy" to illegitimate criticism of Israel's "existence."[11] If we were entering an "age" in which the nation-state was outdated, Michael Walzer demanded, "why start with Israel? Why not with France?... Or [with] the Germans, or the Swedes, or the Bulgarians... all of whom have enjoyed these [national] 'privileges' much longer than Jews."[12] Walzer's rhetorical question implied that Judt's reasoning was infected with anti-Semitism.

Things have changed since then. In February 2016, Thomas Friedman, hardly a radical leftist or an anti-Zionist fanatic, declared in his *New York Times* column: "They all killed the two-state solution. Let the one-state era begin." And he went on: "It's over, folks, so please stop sending the New York Times Op-Ed page editor your proposals for a two-state solution... The next U.S. president will have to deal with an Israel determined to permanently occupy all the territory between the Jordan River and the Mediterranean Sea, including where 2.5 million West Bank Palestinians live."[13]

When Friedman referred in this article to "the next U.S. president," he didn't yet know that would be Donald Trump. Immediately after Trump assumed office, however, Friedman turned to him directly in another op-ed, titled "President Trump, Will You Save the Jews?" According to Friedman, the American president was "the last man standing between Israel and a complete, self-inflicted disaster for the Jewish state and the Jewish people." He observed that Israel was "getting closer every day to wiping out any possibility of a two-state solution," thereby undermining its existence as a country that was, in the words of Moshe Halbertal, "worth defending in moral terms." This situation would "tear apart virtually every synagogue, Jewish organization and Jewish group on every campus in America": "Israel will divide world Jewry."[14] By the end of Trump's presidency, that was in fact what was happening. Peter Beinart's *New York Times* piece "I No Longer Believe in a Jewish State"—and Alan Dershowitz's *Newsweek* response, "Peter Beinart's Final Solution: End Israel as Nation-State for the Jewish People"—made that clear.[15] Two years before, *The New York Times*'s Michelle Goldberg had written an op-ed wondering "Is Liberal Zionism Dead?"[16]

The answer is no, but to get there one must first take note that Israel is very different from a liberal democratic nation-state. Unlike states like France or Sweden, which belong to their citizens, Israel is the state of the Jewish people, not of its citizens as such. The liberalism of liberal Zionism has always had to accommodate the malady of an ethnic distinction, and it is now, after the demise of the two-state solution, that we can see that a truly liberal Zionism—one that's committed to Jewish self-determination in a binational republic—is anything but dead. Indeed, for the first time in Israel's history, a Zionism that is truly liberal has become *necessary*. The future is here: one-state politics now defines Israel's reality, and the consequences are monumental—to Israelis, to Palestinians, and to world Jewry. But we're still lacking a language for liberal Zionist thinking in a post-two-state, post-ethnic era.

The basic vocabulary of this language existed in the past—in Zionism's beginnings. Whereas Zionist politics today is synonymous with the view that Jews have the right to their own sovereign state in Eretz Israel, the movement's founding fathers held a more nuanced view. Intense ideological disagreements divided Herzl, Ahad Ha'am, Jabotinsky, and Ben-Gurion, but they could all agree on the distinction, all too often forgotten, between national self-determination and national sovereignty: up until *very* late in Zionist history, they all viewed the project as committed to the former but *not* the latter. (In fact, they were for the most part committed to the latter's denial.)[17] That is, they believed that the Jews had the right to exercise political self-rule, administrate autonomously their own lives, and revive Jewish culture and education. But they did not believe that this should have been done in a sovereign Jewish state: the Jews' state was envisaged as a sub-sovereign political entity existing under a multinational political sovereignty. Jabotinsky, for example, who is commonly regarded today as a raving right-wing Jewish nationalist, explicitly agreed with Brit Shalom, Martin Buber's Zionist faction, that "the future of Palestine must be founded, legally speaking, as a binational state."[18] Even Hannah Arendt, who is often considered an anti-Zionist, could subscribe to this concept of Zionism. Until late in his career, Ben-Gurion actually did subscribe to it.[19] When Wieseltier or Dershowitz condemn binationalism as a betrayal of Israel and the Jewish people, they overlook the distinction between self-determination and sovereignty: both as a crucial political distinction and as one that, historically, stood at the heart of Zionism's origins. Israel's political survival as a democracy depends on the recovery of this distinction.

3.

Why did the Zionist agenda change from a binational one to that of an ethnic nation-state? The main reason was the Holocaust. The systematic extermination of European Jewry convinced Zionist leaders that Jewish life depended on Jewish sovereignty: on a Jewish military, and on a Jewish polity capable of deciding exclusively on questions of borders and immigration. It also prepared international public opinion for accepting this view. But, in the deepest sense, the Holocaust undermined Jews' trust in a liberal democratic world order. If pluralistic democracy could not protect Jewish life where Jews were a minority, Jews needed their own, exclusive sovereign state. Pluralistic liberalism had to yield to this conclusion not just in Europe, but in Palestine as well.

The second factor, related to the first, was the idea of the Palestinian transfer—that is, of ethnic cleansing—which the British Peel Commission introduced in 1936. Previously, Zionist leaders had no illusions that a tiny Jewish minority could expect to establish its own sovereign state, not even by bringing in waves of Jewish immigration. But once transfer emerged as an actual option, an instant change of mind could be detected in the thinking of Zionist leaders. The idea of a sovereign state, intertwined with that of Palestinian transfer, began to gain currency as the situation of European Jewry deteriorated, and the news of systematic extermination started to arrive. This type of thinking would become actual and concrete in the events of the Nakba.

The Holocaust and the Nakba are thus the main pillars of Zionist thinking as we have come to know it—of the axiom that Zionism is essentially about Jewish sovereignty, and that Jewish demographic superiority, therefore, must be preserved at all costs. It's time to see that this alleged Zionist axiom is not a Zionist axiom at all, and that adhering to it is leading to the destruction of Israel and expulsions of Palestinians.

It is time to restore a binational Zionism—with a strong

notion of equal citizenship in a one-state solution. One way we can do this is by developing an *art of forgetting*, a politics of *remembering to forget* the Holocaust and the Nakba in order to undo rather than perpetuate them as the pillars of future politics.[20] Ernest Renan advanced the idea of such an art of forgetting in his great lecture of 1882, "What Is a Nation?"[21] Renan's account of modern citizenship can help us rethink Israel's future relation to its past. What is true of the Holocaust is true of the Nakba: for the sake of a future binational politics, the systematic expulsion of Palestinians from the country would have to be, in a similar sense, forgotten. But it can be forgotten only if we commemorate it first—and do justice to the past by committing ourselves as citizens to the Palestinians' right of national self-determination. This includes a meaningful commitment to the right of return.

How practical a binational political program would be, one may however wonder. Thoroughly practical. None other than Menachem Begin, Israel's first right-wing prime minister and a vehement opponent of territorial compromise, offers a viable model with the "autonomy plan" he devised in the late 1970s. Begin's program could just as well be called the "one-state plan." It included not only the institution of a Palestinian autonomy in Gaza and the West Bank, but also an option for all Palestinians to become full Israeli citizens, as well as complete freedom of movement and economic rights in Israel, the West Bank, and Gaza; and a department within the Palestinian Autonomy's Council for the Rehabilitation of Refugees. The Knesset voted on this proposal and passed it by a large majority in December 1977.

That Begin had some such plan is familiar to some, but its details, coming so close to a binational constellation, have received little attention. Historians, deferring to the two-state orthodoxy, tend to see the plan as Begin's plot to prevent Palestinian statehood, not as a program that originates in Jabotinsky's binational thinking and could test and open up the ethnic political boundaries and taboos of contemporary Israel.

It is time to explore a program reconstructed from Begin's proposal—I call it the Haifa Republic—recognizing the right of both Jews and Palestinians to national self-determination, even sovereignty, in their own states, separated along the '67 border, and yet regulating their separate sovereignty by a joint constitution ensuring basic human rights, freedom of movement, and economic liberties throughout the territory. Such a plan could allow many settlers to remain in their homes. And it would enable Palestinians to exercise rights commonly associated with the right of return—the aspiration to return to the territories from which they were expelled in 1948. Plans of this sort have been raised in the past, and are still promoted, but they are too often regarded as post-Zionist.[22] The attempt here is to rehabilitate such politics as a Zionist program, consistent with the core aspirations of Zionism's founding fathers.

Ben-Gurion, the ultrapragmatist, is reputed to have once stated, "In order to be realistic in Israel, one has to believe in miracles." This is but a variation on Herzl's original Zionist theme: "If you will it, it is no dream." It is easy to overlook that neither statement is about what these early Zionists allowed themselves to dream, but rather about the concept of *reality* that they assumed when they were the most successful. With the demise of the two-state solution, a realistic democratic politics can only go back to the same audacious view of the world. Sometimes, the alternative to having your mind in the clouds is not having your feet on the ground, but burying your head in the sand.

OMRI BOEHM
Tel Aviv
2021

1

The Liberal Zionism of the Future

The future of Palestine must be founded, legally speaking, as a "binational state."

—ZE'EV JABOTINSKY

1.

IN OCTOBER 2013, the Israeli Supreme Court finally rejected the adjective "Israeli" as an official civil designation in Israel. According to the judges, the claimants who had asked to be labeled "Israeli" rather than "Jewish" on their personal ID cards— did not "sufficiently prove" the existence of an "Israeli nation."[1] For the foreseeable future, therefore, the civil designation of Israel's Jewish citizens remains "Jewish." Arab citizens are often designated "Arab," and sometimes designated "Minority." Putting aside for the moment the irony that an *Israeli* court would make such a decision, the ruling certainly expressed the consensus shared by Israel's Jewish citizens: The state of Israel is, and ought to remain, Jewish. Indeed, Zionists nowadays take it for granted that the existence of a Jewish state in Palestine is what Zionism is essentially about.

But then, can a state be both Jewish and a liberal democracy? And is it true that Zionism necessarily consists in supporting the idea of a Jewish state? A worthwhile future for Israel depends on realizing that the answer to both questions is negative. A Jewish state cannot be a liberal democracy, but the Zionist ambition for Jewish national self-determination is best preserved in a state that is not Jewish. Zionism's early leaders from Herzl to Ben-Gurion understood that fact, one that current liberal Zionist thinkers have managed to repress.

Perhaps the clearest articulation of the current liberal Zionist position is that of the Israeli philosopher Moshe Halbertal. In an influential *Haaretz* article, he dismisses the question of whether a Jewish state can be a liberal democracy as irrelevant: there is no "big question whether a state can be both Jewish and a liberal democracy," he writes; a serious political intellectual debate should turn rather on the question of *"what kind of a Jewish state we want to have"* (my emphasis).[2] It is worthwhile to return to

Halbertal's essay, so eloquent and yet, in its understanding of liberal Zionism, so severely flawed.

Is the notion of a Jewish liberal democracy self-contradictory? To answer that question, Halbertal writes, one must first "find out what a Jewish state is":

> It is possible, of course, to ascribe the adjective "Jewish" a nationalistic or a religious fundamentalist meaning, and then to argue that a [Jewish democratic] combination is impossible, but this would be a circular argument, and not very fruitful.

The charge of circularity is correct, but somewhat misleading. The question at stake is rather whether any definition of the adjective "Jewish," and any definition of who's Jewish and who's not, would allow for a Jewish state that's also a liberal democracy. This question isn't posed by Halbertal quite so clearly, but his answer to it does emerge from the text. The answer is a familiar one: Judaism (obviously) need not be understood as a fundamentalist religion or as nationalist ideology; it can also be interpreted as a pluralistic cultural identity. In Halbertal's view, cultural neutrality is not necessary for democratic liberalism—he believes in the existence of a "right to culture." Therefore, he argues, there is no contradiction in the notion of a liberal Jewish state.

In an earlier paper written with Avishai Margalit, "Liberalism and the Right to Culture," Halbertal had argued that "human beings have a right to culture—*not just any culture, but their own*" (my emphasis).[3] Because one's personality is determined, among other things, by one's particular culture, Halbertal and Margalit argue that one has the right to preserve this culture and ensure its flourishing. In light of this right, it is furthermore the sovereign's duty to protect culture not in some cosmopolitan sense, but in its distinct particularity, taking off the gloves of cultural neutrality that sometimes characterize liberal democracies. According to Halbertal and Margalit, "the right to culture in a liberal state permits the state to be [culturally] neutral, if at all, only with respect to the dominant culture of the majority," and only "on the assumption that the dominant culture can take care of itself."[4] In his *Haaretz* article, Halbertal applies this same logic to the question of Zionism: while it is Israel's obligation to defend the right of its minorities to their own cultures, it is also its right—in fact, its duty—to defend the majority's right to Judaism. From this perspective, he writes, there is no difference between Israel and other culturally non-neutral European democracies, such as "Denmark, Finland, Norway, Germany, the Czech Republic, and more."

However, whereas Judaism is no doubt a culture, belonging to it still requires what one might regard as the opposite of culture: nature, or blood. Religious Jews commonly subscribe to this ethnic condition, as do secular Jews, including those to whom religious Judaism is completely passé. Therefore, the comparison between a Jewish and, say, a Finnish state is idle. Even if there is no contradiction in the notion of a Finnish or German democracy, there is one in the notion of a Jewish democracy, for even if cultural neutrality is not necessary for democratic liberalism, ethnic neutrality certainly is. Quite simply, it is possible to be a Finnish or a Norwegian Jew, just as it is possible to be a German Jew or a Palestinian Christian. But for logical rather than merely political reasons it is impossible to become a Christian or a Muslim Jew. (It is true that one could also convert to Judaism. But even if Israel recognized the progressive conversion practices of Reform Judaism, religious conversion would hardly be an acceptable civil bypass of the ethnicity condition imposed by the Jewish state.)

Neither is it possible to be a Muslim or a Christian *Israeli*, and not merely because Israel's Supreme Court has rejected the existence of an Israeli nation or the adjective "Israeli" as a civil identification. As long as Israel is essentially a Jewish state, being Jewish is essential to being Israeli. A non-Jew can be an Israeli citizen, of course, and carry a blue identification card and passport, but she or he would not for all that *be* Israeli; the state would not for all that *belong* to him or her. It is tempting to liberal Zionist authors to dismiss this distinction as a "confused" subtlety, and to dismiss the notion of a state "belonging" to a people as "unclear,"[5] but nothing here is confused, subtle, or requires much further explanation. When Abraham Lincoln described democracy at Gettysburg as a "government of the people, by the people, for the people," he expressed the basic idea that, in a democracy, sovereignty lies in the people's hands. In a Jewish state, "the people" designates Jews rather than citizens, regardless of religion and race. There is no getting around the fact that a Jewish democracy is, therefore, a "government of the Jews, by the Jews, and for the Jews." It is hard to imagine that any current Zionist, liberal or not, would deny that Zionism as we know it is bound to the idea that Jews have the right to their own sovereignty.

In this light, the analogy between the political standing of (say) an Italian Jewish minority and an Arab minority in Israel is futile. Jews in Italy are integrally included in their state's political identity, and would be insulted if anyone questioned their belonging to the sovereign Italian people. Arabs in Israel are—to put it simply—not part of the sovereign Jewish people.[6] The essence of a liberal democracy, however, is that the sovereign people gives rights to themselves—the only question is who belongs to the people. Consider again Halbertal's claim that there is "no big question" whether a state can be Jewish and democratic; the question is only "what kind of a Jewish state we want to have [in Israel]." The most telling word here is "we," for it obviously designates the

Jews. Arabs aren't included in these deliberations about what kind of Jewish state *we* want to have in *our* country, and if there is no contradiction in the notion of a Jewish liberal democracy, then there isn't one in the notion of a liberal democratic ethnocracy. You cannot square a circle, but generations of Israeli philosophers and public intellectuals have pretended that they can.

Take, for example, David Grossman's much-acclaimed speech on Israel's Memorial Day, 2018.[7] He spoke of Israel's tragedy by saying that Israelis are "not yet home." The state of "Israel was established," he said, "so that the Jewish people, who have nearly never felt at-home-in-the-world, would finally have a home. And now, 70 years later, strong Israel may be a fortress, but it is not yet a home." And, Grossman continued,

> when Israeli snipers kill dozens of Palestinian protesters, most of them civilians—Israel is less of a home....
>
> When it neglects and discriminates against 1.5 million Palestinian citizens of Israel; when it practically forfeits the great potential they have for a shared life here—it is less of a home—both for the minority and the majority.
>
> And when Israel strips away the Jewishness of millions of Reform and Conservative Jews—again it becomes less of a home.

"The solution to the great complexity of Israeli-Palestinian relations can be summed up in one short formula," he said, namely the two-state solution: "If the Palestinians don't have a home, the Israelis won't have a home either." Fifteen years ago, such talk of a simple formula may have been reasonable. But times change, and the once-beautiful words are now sliding into dangerous kitsch. This danger was evident in Grossman's use of the metaphor of "home." It may sound nice, perhaps, to speak of the State of Israel as a "home" to the Jews. A home is private and cozy, belongs to the family, and depends on relations of kinship and love. That's exactly how Israelis do think of their state, but liberal democracies are actually anything but such a home. Liberal states should be public rather than private; should belong to citizens as such rather than a people conceived as a family; and should depend on a neutral, blind legal system—ensuring the rule of law—not on relations of blood or love. The familiar tendency to think of Israel as the Jews' *own* home—in that sense, their private state—cannot be separated from the conviction that they have the right to expel, occupy, and discriminate against all those who do not belong to the family. When Grossman states that as long as the "Palestinians don't have a home, the Israelis won't have a home either," he clearly means by "Israelis" Israeli *Jews*. By the same token, if Palestinians living in Israel were to live in their own home, it could only be in the Palestinian state. It is high time for intellectuals of Grossman's and Halbertal's stature to help Israelis overcome the simplistic idea of the Jews' own home, and allow them to imagine Jewish self-determination, not sovereignty, within a neutral, and so genuinely liberal, republic: a state belonging to all citizens as such.

2.

In the aftermath of Trump's rise to power, the contradictions inherent within the idea of an ethnic liberal democracy have become unignorable—if not in Israel then for the next generation of liberal American Jews. On the one hand, a large majority of American Jews could rightly take pride in a powerful liberal tradition stretching back to such models as Louis Brandeis—a defender of social justice and the first Jew to become a Supreme Court justice—or Rabbi Abraham Joshua Heschel, who marched in Selma alongside the Reverend Dr. Martin Luther King, Jr. On the other hand, Jewish communities often identify themselves with Zionism, which cannot but consist in ethnic and religious separation.

To appreciate this inherent tension, consider Hillary Clinton's words from the second US presidential debate of 2016: "It is important for us as a policy not to say, as Donald has said, we're going to ban people based on a religion. How do you do that?

We are a country founded on religious freedom and liberty."[8] Here Clinton establishes a minimum standard of liberal decency that few American Jews would be inclined to deny. But she was not elected president, and Trump's willingness to reject this standard rightly became a cause for alarm among Jewish communities, along with those of other American minorities.

Yet insofar as Israel is concerned, every liberal Zionist has not just tolerated the denial of this minimum liberal standard, but avowed it as core to their innermost convictions. Whereas liberalism depends on the idea that states must remain neutral on matters of religion and race, Zionism, as we have seen, consists in the idea that the State of Israel belongs to the Jewish people. As long as liberalism was secure back in the United States and the rejection of liberalism was confined to the Israeli scene, this tension could be mitigated. But as it spills out into the open in the rapidly changing landscape of American politics, the double standard is proving difficult to defend.

That difficulty was especially visible at Texas A&M University in 2016, when Richard Spencer, the ideological leader of the alt-right's white nationalist agenda—which he has called a sort of "white Zionism"[9]—was publicly challenged by the university's Hillel rabbi Matt Rosenberg to study with him the Jewish religion's message of "radical inclusion and love."[10]

"Do you really want radical inclusion into the State of Israel?"

Spencer replied. "Maybe all of the Middle East could go move in to Tel Aviv or Jerusalem. Would you really want that?" Spencer went on to argue that Israel's ethnic-based politics was the reason Jews had a strong, cohesive identity, and that Spencer himself admired them for it. The rabbi could not find words to answer, and his silence reverberated through thousands of Twitter views and newspaper commentaries. Later, Rosenberg apologetically explained that he wasn't on his "high school debate team,"[11] but poor rhetorical skills can hardly explain his silence. A David Grossman, Moshe Halbertal, or, say, Michael Walzer could not have answered any better, since the only answer is to embrace a double standard.

Right-wing politicians and commentators in the United States have been putting pressure on this double standard for years. In her 2015 book, *¡Adios, America!: The Left's Plan to Turn Our Country Into a Third World Hellhole*, the commentator Ann Coulter writes:

> Palestinians demand a right to return to their pre-1967 homes, but Israel says, quite correctly, that changing Israel's ethnicity would change the idea of Israel. Well, changing America's ethnicity changes the idea of America, too. Show me in a straight line why we can't do what Israel does. Is Israel special? For some of us, America is special, too.[12]

Coulter gets her dates mixed up. Palestinians in fact do not demand a right of return to their pre-1967 homes, but to their pre-1948 homes. In other words, the issue isn't the occupation, which many liberal Zionists agree is a crime, but the Nakba, the significance of which liberal Zionists commonly strive to repress. Opposition to the Palestinians' right of return to the homes from which they were expelled is a matter of consensus among left and right Zionists because so-called liberals also insist that Israel has the right to ensure that Jews constitute the ethnic majority in *their* country. Jews worldwide are encouraged to "return" to Israel and be immediately naturalized, while a Palestinian return to lands from which they have been expelled is taboo.

It is sometimes suggested that the Jews' ethnicity-based right of return is not an anomaly in liberal nation-states. The philosopher Andrew Pessin, for example, contends that "*many* countries have similar laws favoring or expediting citizenship for descendants of those who originally came from those places, including many European countries such as Germany, Hungary and Italy."[13] This is an awkward comparison, for if Israel were to adopt a law of this kind, it would expedite the Palestinians' right of return to the territories from which they were driven out: it might even accord them preferential treatment. The European provisions that Pessin mentions are exactly what liberal Zionists continue to vehemently oppose, because they would threaten the

Jewish state's Jewish demography. After all, there was a reason why the Palestinians had to be expelled in the first place. In the end, this is what the Jews' right to "culture" amounts to. It is also the reason why Rabbi Rosenberg could not answer Richard Spencer. And yet anyone who questions this underlying double standard will be denounced by organizations such as the American Israel Public Affairs Committee or the Jewish Federations of North America as anti-Semitic.

This incoherent and, finally, illiberal Zionism is all the more pernicious because it is continuous with—rather than in opposition to—the anti-Semitic politics of the sort promoted by the alt-right. The idea that Israel is the Jews' own ethnic state implies that Jews living outside of it—say, in America or in Europe—enjoy a merely diasporic existence. That is another way of saying that they inhabit a country that is not genuinely their own. Given this logic, it is natural for Zionist and anti-Semitic politicians to find common principles and interests. Every American who has been on a Birthright Israel tour will recognize that even left-leaning Israelis can agree with America's alt-right and Europe's anti-Semites that, ideally, "Jews should live in their own country."

This continuity is natural, and it has a long and significant history. When Heinz-Christian Strache, the leader of Austria's far-right Freedom Party, visited Israel in 2016, he was embraced by top members of Benjamin Netanyahu's coalition.[14] Strache's party currently advances policies that are largely anti-Islam and anti-immigration. It was founded, however, by former Austrian Nazis, and Jörg Haider, a former leader of the party, was infamous for showing sympathy for some of Hitler's policies. Another case in point is Geert Wilders, a xenophobic far-right Dutch politician. In December 2016 it was revealed that Wilders's visits to Israel and his meetings with Israeli personnel had been so frequent that the Dutch intelligence community investigated his "ties to Israel and their possible influence on his loyalty."[15]

The close ties between American fundamentalist evangelical Christians—whose views of the Jews' place in the larger messianic scheme is flatly anti-Semitic—and the State of Israel is another case in point, and under Trump, this collaboration between right-wing Zionism and the anti-Semitic alt-right was introduced into the heart of American politics. Neither Israeli nor American Zionist leaders criticized Stephen K. Bannon's appointment as the White House's chief strategist. To the contrary, they publicly and unequivocally welcomed the possibility of working with one of the most powerful ideologues of the alt-right. Alan Dershowitz, the outspoken Harvard emeritus professor of law who regularly denounces non-Zionists as anti-Semites, turned not against Bannon but against his critics. "It is not legitimate to call somebody an anti-Semite because you might disagree with their politics," he pointed out.[16]

"Jews will not replace us" was the slogan of the 2017 Charlottes-ville Unite the Right march. The American president responded to this open show of anti-Semitism—accompanied by Nazi flags—by speaking of the "very fine people" who had participated in it, while blaming what he called the "alt-left."[17] Meanwhile, Prime Minister Netanyahu remained silent. In the aftermath of the Pittsburgh Tree of Life Synagogue shooting, Ron Dermer, Israel's ambassador in Washington, made a similar claim, clearly instructed by Netanyahu. He accused "both sides"—that is, lib-eral critics of Israel, inevitably including liberal Jews like those murdered at the synagogue—of anti-Semitism.[18]

How far can such unholy alliances go? In 1941 Avraham "Yair" Stern, the leader of the right-wing Zionist paramilitary group Lehi and one of the ideological fathers of Netanyahu's Likud party, wrote a letter to Nazi high officials. In it, Stern proposed teaming up with "Herr Hitler" on "solving the Jewish question" by achieving a "Jewish-free Europe." The solution could be achieved, Stern continued, through the "settlement of these masses in the home of the Jewish people, Palestine." To that end, he offered to collaborate with the German's "war efforts," and establish a "Jewish state on a national and totalitarian basis, bound by treaty with the German Reich."[19]

It has been convenient to ignore the existence of Stern's letter, just as it has been convenient to downplay the underlying thinking behind it. Today, however, when the sanctification of Zionism has reached a point where it condones nationalist, anti-Semitic politics, we cannot afford to ignore this letter, which bares a logic that is still very much at work. It is this logic that a new, truly liberal Zionism must regret and uproot.

3.

Moshe Halbertal, in his *Haaretz* article, offers two criteria for judging whether a nation-state is "liberal democratic" rather than "fascist nationalist." The first is whether the state's character as a nation-state "harms the political, economical, or cultural rights" of minorities. The second is whether the state "would support and grant the right of self-definition and determination of other national groups living inside it." These criteria are significant, but their presentation in this context is misleading. While it is true that the liberalism of nation-states can be evaluated by the way they treat minorities, the Jewish state isn't, as we have seen, a liberal democratic nation-state in the same way as common European countries are. Italy may be more or less successful in giving rights to minorities, but these minorities are *Italian*; giving them rights doesn't threaten the idea of an Italian democracy. Since Arabs in the Jewish state certainly aren't a Jewish minority, their presence in the country does threaten the idea of a Jewish democracy. That is why the majority of them were forced out of the country to begin with.

To claim that a Jewish state *could* be liberal in the future if it granted non-Jews their full rights is to claim that a Jewish state could have related to Arabs differently from the way it has in the last seventy years. And, indeed, that it could in principle do so in the future. But it couldn't, and cannot. The claim that it could constitutes the deepest betrayal of liberal principles by today's liberal Zionists. It is important to see why.

It is an axiom of liberal politics that in order to defend citizens' rights, political power must be restrained—because where the power of government can be abused, it will be. Checks and balances, the separation of branches of government and of church and state, and the commitment to a binding constitution are deemed *necessary* to prevent powerful individuals, classes, and groups from abusing their power, taking control of the state, and robbing the people of their sovereignty. The idea, however, that Jews in a Jewish democracy, expressing Jewish sovereignty, would *grant* non-Jews their rights is as untenable in theory as it has proved to be in practice. If the idea held up, liberal democracies wouldn't be required at all. It would make much more sense to let a wise, just sovereign govern, and trust that he would do a better job at ensuring rights than the voting multitudes. This logic has of course been familiar at least since the philosopher-king of Plato's *Republic*, but it is hardly liberal. It is time to admit that the Jewish people wouldn't give non-Jews their rights in their own state any more than a benevolent tyrant would give people their rights in his. A worthwhile future in Israel, not just for Arabs but also for Jews—something Plato did get right is that ruling over others is not good for the soul—demands that we end any self-deception on this score.

To see the consequences of such self-deception, consider the recently legislated quasi-constitutional Basic Law: Israel, the Nation State of the Jewish People, in relation to the country's Declaration of Independence. For the first seventy years of Israel's existence, its identity as both Jewish and democratic was defined by the declaration's pledge that the Jewish state would ensure "complete equality... irrespective of religion, race or sex."[20] This foundational text also carefully leaves open the idea that the Palestinians would exercise national self-determination. It characterizes the Jews' right to determine their destiny as akin to that of "all other nations" and mentions that the Jewish state would be established *in*—not *over*—Eretz Israel.

The Declaration of Independence has often been celebrated as a beacon of liberal Zionist politics, but the truth about it has always been messier and uglier. The declaration's openness to Palestinian national self-determination on the one hand and its pledge to ensure their individual equality on the other has always depended on a conditional relation, a quid pro quo. Arabs can be equal (in individual rights) within the Jewish state so long as national sovereignty remains with Jews. In a democracy, such sovereignty is guarded by ensuring sufficient superiority in numbers. Insofar as Palestinian self-determination is confined to territory outside Israel, it sustains Jewish demographic superiority within Israel and is therefore acceptable. This is still the main argument in favor of a two-state solution on the Zionist left.

From this perspective, despite appearances, the new nation-state law does not contradict Israel's Declaration of Independence. It only makes explicit the fact that Arabs' rights have been, in a Jewish state, conditional, and that the conditions under which Arabs' rights align with Jews' interests no longer obtain. For some time now, it's been an open secret that there will be no two-state solution, and that Israel has claimed for itself the whole of Palestine's territory. Accordingly, the nation-state law asserts that "the right to self-determination" in the country is "unique to the Jewish People," and flouts the pledge to universal equality, specifying that the "development of Jewish settlement" is from now on "a national value."[21] Once the commitment to the partition of Palestine and to Palestinian self-determination outside Israel is explicitly given up, Palestinians again constitute about 50 percent of Israel's population. The declaration's pledge to uphold individual equality "irrespective of religion, race or sex" cannot then be sustained. The point of this law is to put in place the legal infrastructure for future annexations.

In that light, the consequences of the discriminatory clause supporting "Jewish settlement" as a "national value" are monumental. In the ongoing conflict over territory and demography, favoring Jewish settlements is never limited to favoring Jewish interests. It is also actively used to expropriate Arab citizens and Palestinian inhabitants. The methods are familiar nowadays mostly from the West Bank's flourishing settlement project, but they have also been successfully executed within Israel's recognized borders. In the 1980s, numerous Jewish villages were established in the north of the country, as a part of a heavily funded government program called Judaizing the Galilee. (Unlike central and southern Israel, the Galilee remained relatively densely populated by Arabs even after 1948.) The establishment of the Galilee's communal Jewish villages—I grew up in one of them— enabled the government to confiscate the land of Arab Israelis, check the natural growth of their villages, and disrupt territorial continuity between Arab Israeli towns. Since these are communal villages, Arabs are officially not allowed to move in. The new nation-state law lends crucial legal support to such methods, which have been constantly challenged in Israel's Supreme Court.

Proponents of the new law sometimes emphasize that, in contrast to its earlier formulations, the version of the bill that eventually passed doesn't explicitly prioritize Israel's Jewish identity over its democratic character. This is a dodge. The new nation-state law didn't have to openly prioritize Israel's Jewishness over its democratic procedures because another Basic Law, the one regulating the country's elections, already does just that.

Clause 7A of Basic Law: The Knesset specifies that any person or party who in word or deed negates Israel's "Jewish and democratic character" must be banned from running for the Knesset.[22] The spirit behind this clause is the familiar principle of "militant democracy"—roughly, the idea that democracies may legitimately exclude from democratic participation extremist political actors who aspire to abuse elections to undermine democracy from within. Goebbels is reputed to have once stated that the joke about democracy is that it gave its greatest enemies the weapons to destroy it—famously, Hitler took power through elections. The principle of militant democracy is supposed to spoil this "joke."[23]

But where it may be legitimate to exclude antidemocratic parties in order to defend democracy itself, the extension of this principle to defend Israel's Jewish character subverts democracy at its very foundations. It undermines the right for democratic representation in defense not of democracy, but of ethnocracy, and of a particular state ideology, namely Zionism.

The damage that this Basic Law inflicts on Israel's democracy cannot be overstated, but it is often underestimated. It is common among Israelis to make the point that Arab Israelis are obviously allowed to vote in the country, but, in view of this law, Arabs' voting rights are only conditional, and aren't the same as those of Jews. Constituting 22 percent of Israel's citizens, Arab Israelis cannot be expected to support the country's Jewish character any more than African Americans could support the United States as a white country. Arab Israeli representatives are tolerated, but their standing is conditional—the legal basis for their exclusion is already in place—and legally they *cannot* promote the politics that's most important to their voters. For the same reason that the Jewish state drove out its large Arab majority, it must regard the votes of those Arabs who did not flee as potentially subversive: they could "abuse" democracy to oppose the state's Jewish character. But again, this is not a defense of democracy but a prioritization of the Jewishness of the state over democracy. As Ahmad Tibi, an eloquent Arab Israeli member of the Knesset, once pointed out, Israel is indeed both Jewish and democratic: "It is ... in fact democratic for Jews and Jewish for Arabs."[24]

A month before Israel's nation-state law was passed, the Joint List, a parliamentary alliance consisting mostly of Arab Israeli members of the Knesset, proposed a bill of its own, Basic Law: The State of All Its Citizens. It proposed transforming Israel from a Jewish state to a neutral liberal republic. This was a legitimate democratic proposal if there ever was one, but the Knesset did not debate this bill and voted to reject it. Empowered by the aforementioned clause 7A, it exercised its right to ban altogether proposals that question Israel's Jewish character. Unlike the new nation-state law, Basic Law: The Knesset, with clause 7A, is foundational and taken for granted. Liberals may have criticized the new nation-state law as an offense to the Declaration of Independence, but they have no criticism of its pledge to ensure a "Jewish and democratic state."

4.

Halbertal's claim that the liberalism of nation-states is measured by the way they treat their minorities is unsatisfactory for another reason: it overlooks the threats posed to the rights of the majority. One can easily imagine a state of affairs in which the state's violation of religious and ethnic non-neutrality harms the majority no less—and possibly more—than it does the minority. Precisely because one's personality is determined, as Halbertal and Margalit argue, by one's culture, neutrality is crucial to protecting culture from the corrupting power of the state. A Jewish state is hardly the right political entity to ensure Jews' right to their culture. It

43

is no coincidence that their cultural and religious liberties have actually come under fierce attack in the State of Israel.

It is widely known that Reform and Conservative Judaism—the largest, most significant branches of world Jewry—are not recognized as "kosher" in Israel. Their religious practices are seriously constrained. Reform and Conservative rabbis cannot legally perform wedding ceremonies in the country, nor convert believers to Judaism according to their faith: the state officially favors Judaism's Orthodox interpretation, and inhibits the alternatives. Jews' religious liberties are therefore much better protected not only in America, but in, say, Germany, Italy, or Poland than they are in the Jewish state. If any of these countries attacked Jewish religious and cultural freedom as aggressively as Israel does, it would be, with good reason, denounced as anti-Semitic. The point to stress here is that, as in the case of Palestinians' rights, there is nothing surprising or contingent about the fact that rights of Jews come under attack in the Jewish state. State neutrality and the separation of church and state are necessary not only to protect the state from the power of religion, but also to protect religion and culture from the power of the state.

In this case, Israel offends as monumentally against Jewish rights as it does against Arab Israelis' voting rights. A Reform rabbi simply could not work in Israel, because Reform communities aren't free to live according to their faith there. This is something that liberal Zionist Jews in North America know well, but prefer to keep relatively quiet about. In order to preserve Israel's image as a liberal democracy, they are willing to tolerate not just its attack on Palestinians' fundamental rights, but also its attack on the fundamental rights of Jews.

It is, in any case, not Jewish culture that Israel is designed to protect but Jewish ethnicity, Jewish blood. That is what makes it a nationalist, but hardly liberal, project, whose inconsistent character is most clearly explained in its Jewish public education system.

Moshe Halbertal has argued correctly that a state's education system is its most significant political institution, while insisting that there is no inherent problem with a public education system that is officially Jewish. The situation, he writes, "is not different from those of many other modern countries; their public education systems diffuse their own unique cultural identity.... A Jew who is a German citizen, American citizen, or French, will have to finance from his own pocket private Jewish education for his children. In Israel as a Jewish state, such education will be financed by the state." This, however, is misleading. It is true that Jews who are interested in getting a Jewish education for their children in the United States or France finance it out of their own pockets, but so, of course, do Christians. The public education systems in Germany, France, and the United States are German, French, and

45

American—not Christian. There is no reason why Jewish children shouldn't study in a American, French, or German public school, because they are (or could become) American, French, or German. Clearly, however, non-Jewish parents can only send their children to Israel's Jewish education system at the price of forsaking their own culture and religion.

The Jewish education system of the Jewish state is not, as one might suppose, a question of culture. Again, it is one of blood. As my *Bildung* German Jewish grandmother and my traditional Iranian Jewish grandfather must have realized, Israel's Jewish education system wasn't protecting their rich and different Jewish cultures, but mainly their common Jewish ethnicity. It is easy enough to imagine the liberal, public education that strikes a healthy balance between the study of Homer, the Bible, and the Quran; between the study of Bialik and Darwish; between the study of the history of the Holocaust and that of the Nakba. Anyone interested could have privately financed further Jewish, Muslim, or Christian education for their children. Such a civic public school system is inconceivable as things stand, for the simple reason that, if they studied together, Jewish and Arab children would quickly fall in love. Within one generation, they would have children of their own. And indeed, how could a Jewish state handle the mixed sons and daughters of a humanistic education system? Would the Supreme Court approve their designation as Israeli rather than Jewish or Arab? It is one thing for, say, American Jews to worry in private about assimilation and mixed marriages in their own family and community; even to treat it, as Peter Beinart does in his earlier work, as a major social and political problem of Jewish life.[25] Like it or not, the worry can be understood, and tolerated, as long as it remains a private affair. Liberal Zionists ought to agree that the solution to the "problem" of mixed marriages and assimilation is *not* a state that enforces ethnic separations through its education system and other public institutions.

5.

The Jewish state, for these reasons, is not and cannot be a liberal democracy. Does it follow that Zionist politics has to be abandoned?

This conclusion may well seem to follow, given the prevalent assumption that Zionism's very essence is the existence of a Jewish state: that the Zionist idea of securing the Jews' right to national self-determination is synonymous with Jewish sovereignty, and that the Jewish state established on May 14, 1948, is the telos of Zionist political ambitions. The same assumption also guides the stubborn insistence that the circle must be squared: to argue,

47

despite the facts, that there is no question whether a state can be both Jewish and liberal.

Now is a good moment for liberal Zionists to abandon this sanctified false axiom. Jews most certainly do have the right to national self-determination, but the assumption that this right is best defended and can only be defended by a sovereign Jewish state is, to say the least, debatable, and quite probably mistaken. The idea that nations are only supposed to express themselves as sovereign political entities is not a national but a nationalistic idea: it is created not by the desire to protect national rights, but by the wish to elevate the nation as the supreme category—the ultimate arbiter of identity, meaning, and power. And if, instead of sacralizing Jewish nationalism, one wished to defend the actual national and cultural rights of the Jews, a sub-sovereign political autonomy within a constitutional federative structure would serve far better to preserve Jewish education, art, and religion, and the study and status of Hebrew. Such a federative constellation would also better protect the national rights of Palestinians alongside those of the Jews.

A sub-sovereign political entity may sound like a post- or anti-Zionist utopia, and utopian it may well be, but it is certainly fully Zionist. After all, Theodor Herzl's 1902 utopian novel *The Old New Land* envisions the socioeconomic, cultural, and political life of the state of the Jews as a cultural-political autonomy lying side by side with other such autonomies under Ottoman sovereignty. The idea of a fully-fledged Jewish sovereignty was altogether foreign to Herzl's thoughts and dreams, but he was not for all that less of a Zionist.

Most of Herzl's interpreters have considered *The Old New Land*'s autonomy model to be a break from his 1896 Zionist manifesto, *The Jewish State*, and what they take to be its stand for full Jewish sovereignty. *The Old New Land*'s portrayal of the Jewish state as a "mere" autonomous district in Palestine must represent a radical shift in Herzl's thinking, the argument goes, unless, perhaps, it's an attempt to conceal his treasonous ambitions vis-à-vis Palestine's Ottoman rulers.[26] But it's a myth that *The Old New Land* and *The Jewish State* stand for different Zionist visions, a myth created by an ideological (mis)interpretation of Herzl's works from the retroactive perspective of the sovereign Jewish state as eventually established that makes it seem the obvious, necessary end of Zionist politics all along.[27] No break occurred in Herzl's Zionist thinking. When advocates of European nations in Herzl's time—Czechs or Hungarians, say—spoke about attaining their own "states," they had in mind a national territorial autonomy, and national self-determination, under imperial sovereignty. The "state" in *The Jewish State* is the same nonsovereign political entity Herzl would later describe in *The Old New Land*.

Crucially, Herzl rejected the example of what he called the

"new Greece," where, following the rebellion against Ottoman rule in 1821, a culturally and linguistically homogeneous sovereign state had been founded in 1832.[28] The father of political Zionism was utopian rather than messianic: he was not invested in the idea of the Jews' return to their ancient biblical homeland, he opposed the revival of Hebrew as the Jews' historically national language, and his Zionism wasn't nationalistic either: Jewish sovereignty he saw as a golden calf. By today's false Zionist axioms Herzl was an anti-Zionist.

And not just he. The same retroactive ideological distortion is responsible for the common dismissal of Ahad Ha'am's Zionism as "cultural" rather than "political." His Zionism was altogether political: well aware of the existence of a Palestinian people in the land, which others preferred to ignore, he advocated a Jewish cultural autonomy in Palestine, existing alongside a Palestinian autonomy in one binational federation. Unlike Herzl, Ahad Ha'am vehemently supported the revival of Hebrew as the Jews' national language. Unlike Herzl, he wasn't attached to existing empires. And, unlike Herzl, he gave much weight to the presence of the Palestinian people on the territory: he was alert to the main *political* questions that would haunt Zionism for years. On the issue of the Jewish state's sub-sovereign status, however, Ahad Ha'am and Herzl agreed. "The situation," Ahad Ha'am wrote, "makes Palestine a joint home of different nations, each of which is trying to build its own national home":

> In such a situation, it is no longer possible for the "national home" of one of them to be complete and encompass every aspect of this term [i.e., sovereignty]. If you do not go about building your home in a field empty of people, but rather in a place where there are other homes and residents, then of course you can only be the sole ruler inside your own gates. There, inside, you can organize your belongings as you see fit. But beyond your gates, all residents of the area must work together, and the overall leadership must be agreed upon for the benefit of all.[29]

Herzl has been falsely construed as supporting sovereignty, but it was impossible to distort Ahad Ha'am's thinking in this way. Since it was impossible to dismiss him as an anti-Zionist, either, he became a "nonpolitical" Zionist.

In any case, it's widely believed, even by some experts, that binational Zionism of the sort Ahad Ha'am advocated never really had a following. Or, if it did, it was only among the sanctimonious, far-fetched Brit Shalom, of intellectuals such as Martin Buber, Arthur Ruppin, and Judah Magnes. But Brit Shalom's

continuity with Ahad Ha'am's ideas was due mostly to the significance they gave to the revival of Hebrew and Jewish culture—not
to their binational politics, which, up until very late, remained a
matter of consensus among Zionist founding fathers. None other
than Ze'ev Jabotinsky expressed complete agreement with Brit
Shalom's binational plan, which he emphasized ought to be taken
for granted, even as he criticized their desire to announce a Jewish
state when Palestine's Jewish population was still a small minority:

> The future of Palestine must be founded, legally speaking, as a
> "binational state." And not just Palestine. Every land that has an
> ethnic minority, of even the smallest kind, would need, after all,
> according to our deeply held views, to adapt its legal regime to
> that fact and become a bi-tri-national or quatra-national state.[30]

Throughout his career, Jabotinsky supported the idea of a
Nationalitätenstaat as opposed to a *Nationalstaat*: a multinational federation as opposed to a nation-state. After World War
I had brought the collapse of empires and the birth of nations,
Jabotinsky advocated a Jewish state in broader Palestine, and his
sharp opposition to any territorial compromise was backed by
an insistence that the future of the territory would be multinational rather than cut into sovereign nation-states. His 1940 *The*

Jewish War Front, which would be his final and most mature political template, explains that

> the Jewish and the Arab ethno-communities shall be recognized as autonomous public bodies of equal status before the law. . . . Each ethno-community shall elect its National Diet with the right to issue ordinances and levy taxes within the limits of its autonomy, and to appoint a national executive responsible before the Diet.[31]

Nowadays, people would be likelier to associate such a political program with Hannah Arendt, who was considered an anti-Zionist, rather than with Jabotinsky.

Ben-Gurion too was at first committed to an autonomous national district under Ottoman sovereignty. Then, after World War I, he started advocating a sovereign Jewish state, but again one in which both Jews and Palestinians would exercise national self-determination in cultural autonomies. In other words, by sovereignty he seemed to mean binational self-determination, independent from the empires:

> In such a country with such a great multiplicity of races, ethnicities, religions, international political connections, and

socio-cultural doctrines, it is impossible that there could be one law and one arrangement.... Whatever kind of government there will be in Palestine, whether it is a Mandate government or whether it would one day become a government of the inhabitants of Palestine, this makes it necessary for the central national government to minimize itself to only those governmental functions that must naturally be concentrated in one national administration.... And the conclusion is that the situation in the country necessitates an autonomous arrangement for all the many habitations in Palestine, including what is most important for us, namely the autonomous arrangement for the Jewish Yishuv in Palestine.[32]

And he goes on,

We will not be able to be an autonomous territorial nation—
I believe this has become our goal—because our aim is not to rule over others, not to be a ruler nation like all the other ruler nations, our goal is that we be masters of our own fate, no more than that and no less—we will not realize this aspiration if we do not realize it on the level of our daily life.... It makes no difference if we are a minority and others are the majority, or if we are the majority and others are a minority. Just relations

between nations cannot depend on that, on whether one nation is a minority and another is a majority. That is the basic assumption that informs and determines the relations between us and our Arab neighbors. And we must draw all the practical conclusions from this basic assumption.... And that same basic assumption that we adopt for ourselves, it cannot be just for us, but rather it must be a general assumption for the entire population of Palestine, whether they are a majority and we are a minority or we are a majority and they are a minority. All other notions undermine our existence in Palestine.[33]

It is interesting to notice what Ben-Gurion does *not* mean when he emphasizes that it is not the Jews' aim to "rule over others." He does not have in mind, of course, the military occupation of the Palestinians, but the idea that Palestinian citizens will live under Jewish sovereignty, in a Jewish state. Back then, at least, he rejected the Jewish democratic contradiction, hoping for Jews to run their own lives without corrupting themselves into a ruler nation. In this passage, it is not the occupation but Jewish sovereignty that would corrupt Zionism. Autonomy was accordingly the model, and it is because autonomous districts secure self-determination that it makes "no difference" whether the Jews or the Palestinians are the majority or the minority. A hundred years have not yet passed since Ben-Gurion delivered this speech: his prediction that all other types of politics would "undermine our existence in Palestine" may still prove accurate.

In the early 1930s, the principles outlined in this speech were gathered into a quasi-constitutional document, "Assumptions for Determining a Governmental Regime in Palestine." Here Ben-Gurion specifies his vision:

> Palestine would become a federal state whose subsections will be: (1) the municipal government of the village and the city, which is completely independent; (2) cantons that comprise autonomous states within the federal Palestinian government. Every continuous habitation of no less than twenty-five thousand people is able to become a free canton. Every canton is able to write its constitution for itself. No canton can pass a law that restricts or violates the rights and equality of another canton's residents. Every citizen has equal rights in all the cantons; (3) the national autonomy would have complete authority in the areas of education, culture, and language, according to the constitution that would be passed by the founding assembly.[34]

Again, this could come from Arendt. Her essay "To Save a Jewish Homeland," written on the eve of Israel's establishment in 1948, ends with this plea:

Local self-government and mixed Jewish-Arab municipal and rural councils, on a small scale and as numerous as possible, are the only realistic political measures that can eventually lead to the political emancipation of Palestine. It is still not too late.[35]

One almost feels here that Arendt has read Ben-Gurion and is trying to remind her readers what originally his Zionist program was about. Amos Oz, advocating an end to occupation and a return to what he took to be the original, just Zionist concept, dismissed the idea of a multinational federation as a dogmatic, moralistic post-Zionist notion. There are only "six multinational states" worldwide, he liked to say: "Switzerland, Switzerland, Switzerland, Switzerland, Switzerland, and let's not forget, Switzerland."[36] Ben-Gurion and the other fathers of the nation were less cynical. If there will be a liberal Zionism in the future, it will have to look much like the original, all-too-forgotten Zionist concept.

6.

How did the Zionist movement depart from the idea of Jewish self-determination in a binational republic and move to assert the Jews' right to a sovereign ethnic state, one of the sort that

Herzl had rejected as a Jewish "new Greece"? Two factors promoted this late development, which began only in the 1930s,
twelve years before the establishment of Israel, and was consoli-
dated in the 1940s. The first was the publication of Peel's British
Palestine Royal Commission, better known as the Peel Commission. It called for Palestine's partition into two separate states,
and suggested that Britain would transfer Palestinian population
from the territories assigned to the Jewish state. Transfer fantasies
had always existed among Zionists, but not as political or practical possibilities. Ben-Gurion's reaction to the commission was
immediate and radical—the idea of transfer, coupled with Jewish
sovereignty, seized his mind. In his diary, he writes:

> The compulsory transfer of the Arabs from the valleys of the
> proposed Jewish state might give us something which we never
> had. . . . We are being given an opportunity that we never dared
> to dream of in our wildest imaginings. This is more than a state,
> government and sovereignty—this is national consolidation in
> an independent homeland.[37]

When Ben-Gurion speaks of something that he could not
"dream" even in his "wildest imaginings," one should take notice.
After all, dreaming wildly was elevated by Zionist leaders into a

form of ideology. Besides, Ben-Gurion had allowed himself to dream of a Jewish *state* all along. He also calls this state "sovereign." But he means by these terms Jewish self-determination within a binational federation. What Ben-Gurion hadn't dreamt of in his "wildest imaginings" was full sovereignty in an ethnically homogeneous nation-state. Only a few years before, in "Assumptions for Determining a Governmental Regime in Palestine," Ben-Gurion took it for granted that a binational republic was the necessary principle on which the Jewish state would be founded. Back then, it still made "no difference whether we are a minority and others are the majority," or the other way around. The realization that transfer might be possible immediately gave rise to a new dream that would culminate in Jewish sovereignty and expulsions of Palestinians.

A second factor was, of course, the Holocaust. The systematic extermination of European Jewry prepared international public opinion for an exclusively Jewish state. It was clear that not only Jewish wealth and welfare, but Jewish life, required protection, and there were Jewish refugees who stood in immediate need of resettlement and added a powerful impetus to the drive for sovereignty instead of autonomy.

Before, it had been thought that the relation of Jews to non-Jews in Palestine would be like that of non-Jews to Jews in the diaspora. This belief was now stood on its head. If the Jews could not secure their well-being in the diaspora, if in Europe the bond of civilized politics between Jews and non-Jews had been betrayed, then it followed that a sovereign Jewish state was a necessity.

The Holocaust led to a consensus in favor of a binational federation. A new politics of transfer would lead in turn to the Nakba. These are developments that must be undone if we wish to return to the civilized, liberal politics of the original Zionists. Ben-Gurion once said, "'Only thus' is an anti-Zionist expression."[38] In the twenty-first century, Zionists will have to return to this wisdom: abandon the Holocaust-based nation-state axiom, which now can only lead to a repetition of Nakba politics—the idea of transferring Palestinians is already making a comeback—and start developing an unapologetic joint Jewish-Palestinian federation.

But what would it mean to restart what we might call, in tribute to Herzl, an old-new politics? How can the memories of the Holocaust and the Nakba serve not as impediments but as supports to a new binational dream? The answer is that such an old-new politics can be developed through the notion of remembering to forget. Such a politics of forgetting lies at the heart of modern liberalism as developed in Ernst Renan's classic account of the relation between nation and citizen.

For Renan, a nation is nothing but a "daily plebiscite," a continuous referendum: it is not relations of blood, language, or even culture—the marks of premodern belonging—that join a nation's people, but *choosing* to belong.[39] This cannot happen, Renan argues, without an "act of forgetting." That is, citizens' "daily" choice to belong together depends, in large part, on their continuous willingness to forget all that might pull them apart. Diverse memories—individual, political, cultural—give rise to divisive identities, which, however, out of shared civic responsibility, citizens must set aside. The willingness to forget is therefore, for Renan, a patriotic duty: every French citizen "ought to have already forgotten" many things.[40]

Such an act of forgetting, however, is not the same as memory erasure—the type that's familiar from Stalin's attempted elimination of Trotsky's role in the Revolution (or, yes, Israel's attempt to eradicate any recollection of the Nakba). To the contrary, Renan's politics of forgetting is best captured by the idea that citizens must *remember to forget*. History must not be whitewashed or suppressed: it must be recalled and recognized, the better to set these recollections aside. In fact, only where history is firmly remembered can the politics of *continuous* forgetting that is crucial to the "daily referendum" or to choosing to belong take place. It is not, in other words, that history itself, the actual events, are forgotten, but rather that the perspective from which the events are recollected undergoes a fundamental reconsideration. It is then possible for a new interpretation to emerge that reforms and transforms the memories of the nation. Remembering to forget amounts in this sense to remembering the events, but from a different perspective: one that, to speak with Nietzsche, would be healthier for life.

Renan was well aware, for example, that all French students learn about the St. Bartholomew and Midi massacres in school, events that he claims French citizens "ought to have already forgotten."[41] His point is not that they are or should be unaware of the events' occurrence, but that they no longer remember them *as* Catholics or Protestants. They have put those respective perspectives aside, and now remember these events as citizens: regretting the violence between two groups because that violence is inimical to the existence of the now-constituted French nation.[42]

The case of Israel is different in numerous ways, but a comparison is illustrative. A culture and politics of Holocaust commemoration does of course exist in the country. It is taken to be the cornerstone of Israeli society. But because it is assumed as a cornerstone, Israeli citizens remember to remember, but forget to forget. The result is an identity politics (of a sort that in the United States has developed because of the country's failure to properly recall its racist heritage), an identity politics that is sponsored by the state but runs counter to the power of citizenship. It unites Jews *as opposed to* all citizens, promoting nationalism as opposed to patriotism. By the same token, in the Jewish state, Nakba commemoration has no place in political memory. And since the Nakba is not remembered, it also cannot be forgotten. Reviving the old-new Zionist dream of binationalism, reinventing a concept of common citizenship in the country, and securing a truly liberal Israel all depend on our ability to remember to forget: both the Holocaust and the Nakba.

2

Forgetting and Remembering: The Holocaust

Is it possible that the antonym of "forgetting" is not "remembering," but justice?

—Yosef Hayim Yerushalmi

1.

On December 8, 1987, an Israeli truck driver passing through the narrow roads of Jabalya—a Palestinian refugee camp on Gaza's northern outskirts—lost control of his vehicle, crashed into two taxis, and killed four Palestinians. The accident, innocent if tragic, was interpreted on the streets as a deliberate attack, unleashing unprecedented popular riots that quickly spread throughout Gaza, the West Bank, and East Jerusalem. The Intifada—back then, it had not yet been dubbed "the First Intifada"—would not cease until September 1993, when Yitzhak Rabin and Yasser Arafat signed the Oslo Accord at the White House. By that time, the Intifada had revolutionized Israeli thinking for years to come.

The most obvious change was political, and its effects could be detected almost immediately. Nearly overnight, the Intifada shattered Israelis' long-held belief in the idea of "enlightened occupation": roughly, the belief that Israel's military regime was humane; that being ruled by Israeli Jews actually benefited the Palestinians; and that, therefore, the occupation was morally defensible and politically sustainable. The enlightened occupation doctrine, a piece of colonialist bad faith if there ever was one, had dominated mainstream Zionist politics for at least two decades. Its rapid disappearance in the late 1980s led to a monumental shift. When the Intifada first broke out, so-called liberal Zionists like Rabin would have dismissed a two-state solution, much as today liberal Zionists dismiss the one-state solution as deluded radicalism. When the riots first erupted, Rabin, who would be assassinated in 1995 for shaking Arafat's hand, still denounced negotiations with the Palestine Liberation Organization (PLO) as treason. Only after the Intifada tore off the mask of the "enlightened occupation" did two-state politics begin to acquire its current sacrosanct status.

The other monumental shift was moral rather than political, and Rabin, who would negotiate with Arafat, was its icon, too. Pressed by journalists about the military's inability to contain the riots, Rabin answered that the IDF would crush them by "breaking the arms and legs" of Palestinians caught throwing stones.[1]

His words were not a direct command or official policy, but they were not intended or interpreted figuratively, either. Soon thereafter, Israeli soldiers were seen on television using large stones to break the limbs of handcuffed young Palestinians. There was no Internet or YouTube back then, but Israel had only one TV channel: everybody saw what happened, and at that point, we were not yet familiar with violent images of the occupation, not yet numbed by habit. Nobody was prepared to deal with such footage. For a split second, Israelis, who preferred to perceive themselves as victims, discovered the discrepancy between their moral reality and the myth of their powerlessness. For a rare moment, we actually *saw* what it looks like when Jews in uniform are perpetrators, not victims.

Some four months after the riot's beginning, a short opinion piece appeared in *Haaretz*: "In Praise of Forgetting."[2] Its author, Yehuda Elkana, a prominent philosophy professor from Tel Aviv University who survived Auschwitz at the age of ten, argued that teaching Israeli children to remember is instilling a dangerous doctrine of hate. Without the "Holocaust's insertion so deeply into [our] national consciousness," he wrote, our political prospects would look different and the IDF's military rule over the Palestinians "would not have produced so many 'exceptional' deeds." By "exceptional," Elkana meant "barbaric." And by putting the word in scare quotes, he warned *Haaretz* readers that barbarism can become the *rule*—that is, not exceptional at all. At a moment of drastic transition he was also warning readers that the country would be unable to rise to the challenges posed by its future without assuming a more mature relation to its past.

The current moment is similar to that one, and arguably more dramatic. The two-state solution, having become as unquestionable as it had been unthinkable, no longer answers the country's political predicaments, and Elkana's warning is more timely than ever. A politics leaning so extensively on the Jewish past, he argued, can only lead to "disastrous consequences." In fact, he warned that there is "no greater danger to Israel's existence" than the "Holocaust's memory":

[In the last weeks] I understand, for the first time, the seriousness of what we've been doing when, decade after decade, we sent every Israeli child on repeated visits to Yad Vashem.... We declaimed, insensitively and harshly, and without explanation: *Remember! Zachor!* To what purpose? What is the child supposed to do with these memories? Many of the pictures of those horrors can be interpreted as a call to hate.... Every nation, including the Germans, will decide their own way whether they want to remember or not. For our part, we must learn to forget.

On first look, this argument may seem awkward. Isn't it obvious that memory is necessary for the survival of liberal democracy, that civilized society can only fight the return of barbarism by making sure that we never forget? Especially today, as racist, populist, and nationalist leaders are on the rise worldwide, it is commonplace among liberal thinkers to insist that we must learn from the horrors of the past. A Holocaust survivor may be forgiven for wishing to forget, but Elkana's "In Praise of Forgetting"—which, by now, has achieved quasi-classical status in some circles of the left—may seem not just awkward but outright dangerous.

We have grown accustomed to see memory as a civil duty, however, so it is interesting to notice that Elkana's praise of forgetfulness actually has on its side a long intellectual tradition that's rather suspicious of memory's political function. Spinoza may be the most obvious example. This radical proponent of enlightenment and democracy viewed memory as a major threat to civilized politics. He believed that whereas rational thinking unites people by identifying their true, common interests, memory divides them—attaching them to variety of false identities, misleading myths, and fabricated religions and ideologies. Memory, for Spinoza, is the origin of conflict, violence, and war, never of enlightenment, democracy, or peace.[3]

As is often the case, Nietzsche's insights are continuous with Spinoza's, but formulated more luridly. Those who begin by "looking backwards" will end up thinking backwards, he warns.[4] For the author of "On the Use and Abuse of History to Life," memory is prone to functioning as an "angry spectator." Those who live by memory rather than by the will to forget necessarily become replete with resentment—the "will's ill will toward time and its 'it was.'" They seek "revenge" because they cannot "run backward[s]"—it's always too late to do something about the past—and punish all those who can suffer in the present.[5] Nietzsche isn't often considered much of a liberal democratic political thinker, but his thinking here is not only near contemporary with but close to Renan's claim that modern citizenship depends on an act of forgetting.

Elkana's argument is similar to those of Spinoza and Nietzsche, whether or not he was drawing on them. Israeli democracy was in danger, he claimed, because the state was more attached to memories of past extermination than it was to its present and future interests: such was "Hitler's tragic victory."[6] Modern democratic societies are ruled by economic, social, psychological, and ideological considerations—the building blocks of a compromise born of open, rational exchange—but Israelis are motivated by "deep existential *Angst.*" For too long, Israel's public has been governed by a "certain interpretation of the Holocaust," a mythical, metaphysical account of anti-Semitism according to which "the whole world is against us," and we are "the eternal victim." By constantly presenting politics as a zero-sum game, such existential *Angst* was, for Elkana, inimical to democracy:

> Democracy's very existence is endangered when the memory of past victims takes an active part in the democratic procedure. The ideologists of fascist regimes understood this well. It is no coincidence that most of the research of Nazi Germany concentrates on the myths of the Third Reich.... Using the suffering of the past as a political argument is as good as letting the dead participate in the democratic decisions of the living.

Elkana's challenge hit a nerve, then as now, because political, metaphysical *Angst* has led Israelis to slip from adducing the Holocaust as a political argument to viewing Zionism as a sort of *Angst*-based mythical Holocaust messianism. In Hebrew, this sacralized myth is expressed by the slogan *mi'shoa le'tkuma*: "from Holocaust to resurrection." It captures the widespread conviction that the Third Reich's Jewish victims were no *mere* victims: they were sacrifices—in Hebrew, "victim" and "sacrifice" are the same word, *korban*—in a teleological process that led to the creation of a Jewish state. Viewed in this way as a mythical rather than political entity, Israel transcends the realm of modern, more or less rational, democratic politics.

2.

One of the most shattering testimonies in Elie Wiesel's *Night* describes the execution of a young child, a "sad-eyed angel" with a "delicate and beautiful face."[7] The scene is unforgettable. Caught participating in a sabotage attempt, the child refuses to collaborate with his SS interrogators, remains resolute under torture, and is eventually hanged alongside two other Jewish inmates:

> All eyes were on the child. He was pale, almost calm, but he was biting his lips as he stood in the shadow of the gallows....
>
> The three condemned prisoners together stepped onto the chairs. In unison, the nooses were placed around their necks.
>
> "Long live liberty!" shouted the two men.
>
> But the boy was silent.

"Where is merciful God, where is He?" someone behind me was asking.

At the signal, the three chairs were tipped over....

Then came the march past the victims. The two men were no longer alive. Their tongues were hanging out, swollen and bluish. But the third rope was still moving: the child, too light, was still breathing...

And so he remained for more than half an hour, lingering between life and death.... He was still alive when I passed him. His tongue was still red, his eyes not yet extinguished.

Behind me, I heard the same man asking: "For God's sake, where is God?"

And from within me, I heard a voice answer:

"Where He is? This is where—hanging here from this gallows."[8]

Here lies the beginning of Wiesel's political theology—and his relation to Zionist politics. Here he echoes the biblical narrative of the binding of Isaac, in which God tests Abraham's faith by commanding him to sacrifice Isaac, his only beloved son, as a "burnt offering." *Ola*, the Hebrew term for "burnt offering," describes a sacrifice that must be burnt on the altar, and gives rise to the Greek equivalent "holocaust."

In the story of the binding of Isaac, the child is saved from immolation by the angel of Yahweh: "Do not lay your hand on the lad," he shouts to Abraham, "or do anything to him, for now I know that you fear God."[9] Given that the future existence of Israel as a nation depends on the survival of Abraham's "only beloved son," the whole nation is saved from holocaust through the angel's miraculous intervention at the very last moment. Drawing on a long Jewish tradition, Wiesel maintains that not only Abraham but also God is tested in this story. Will he allow the child's sacrifice? While in the biblical narrative God passes the test—hardly, but he does—in Auschwitz, He does not.[10] No angel appears at the last moment to stop the child's sacrifice. Or, if there was an angel on the scene, it was that dark-eyed child, hanging on the gallows. For Wiesel, Jewish faith died in Auschwitz together with that child. God failed the test by allowing his people's holocaust.

François Mauriac, the Nobel laureate and committed Catholic wrote a foreword to *Night*'s first edition that recounted his meeting with the young Wiesel, and referred back to the execution of the child. Perhaps unsurprisingly, he sees God's death as the beginning of a theology:

What answer was there to give my young interlocutor whose dark eyes still held the reflection of the angelic sadness that had appeared one day on the face of a hanged child? . . . Did I speak

73

to him of that other Jew, this crucified brother who perhaps resembled him and whose cross conquered the world? Did I explain to him that what had been a stumbling block for *his* faith had become a cornerstone for *mine*? And that the connection between the cross and human suffering remains, in my view, the key to the unfathomable mystery in which the faith of his childhood was lost? And yet, Zion has risen up again out of the crematoria and the slaughterhouses. The Jewish nation has been resurrected from among its thousands of dead. It is they who have given it new life.[11]

A Jewish reader could, and perhaps should, perceive Mauriac's foreword as an impolite imposition of Christian theology on Jewish victims. He does not recognize the *contrast* between the Jews' binding of Isaac, in which God passes the test by preventing the child's sacrifice, and Auschwitz, where God fails by allowing the child to burn, as the Holocaust's ultimate theological meaning. Instead, he treats the collapse of Jewish faith as a stepping stone to Christianity. He interprets the Holocaust as a moment that reveals the *similarity* between Auschwitz and the *sacrifice* of Isaac, as Genesis 22 is commonly called in Christian European languages, by contrast to Hebrew. For Christians, Genesis 22 only prefigures Jesus's crucifixion, where the "beloved son" is actually sacrificed, hanging on the cross not unlike Wiesel's sad-eyed angel. But Jesus is subsequently resurrected, and one might think (or so Mauriac hints) that Christianity succeeds exactly where it needs to succeed—that is, where Jewish faith has failed and died—*in giving meaning to Jewish suffering*. Mauriac was enough of a mensch not to state this thought quite so clearly. But the suggestion—it is more than a suggestion, it is a insinuation—is there: Wiesel should have emerged from Auschwitz not as an atheist Jew, but as a devout Christian. And perhaps not only he.

If Wiesel, the proud Jew that he was, was anything but offended, then this is because Mauriac's maneuver can be conveniently interpreted not just as a Christian temptation but also as a Jewish temptation to transform Judaism into Zionist Holocaust messianism. God dies on the gallows, and God is subsequently resurrected: for Wiesel *and* Mauriac, "Zion has risen up again." This is the exact meaning of the Holocaust as it is taught to Israelis, and is the assumed cornerstone of Israeli politics. *Mi'shoa le'tkuma*: from Holocaust to resurrection. Wiesel did not emerge from Auschwitz a Christian, nor quite an atheist Jew. He emerged from it a firm believer in Zionism as the Holocaust's ultimate messianic theology. At times, he would serve as this theology's outspoken prophet.

Such Holocaust messianism has corrupted the Jewish conscience by placing the Jewish state above the realm of universal morality. "I swore never to be silent whenever, wherever human

75

beings endure suffering and humiliation," Wiesel explained in his Nobel acceptance speech. "Neutrality helps the oppressor, never the victim. Silence encourages the tormentor, never the tormented."[12] And Wiesel lived up to his words. From early on, and well before it was easy, or fashionable, he spoke out against South African apartheid, as he did against hate crimes against African Americans. But Israel was different. He never criticized the country's elaborate settlement project, or its decades-long military oppression of the Palestinians. He never objected to Begin's 1982 invasion of Lebanon, and did not speak out when the Sabra and Shatila massacres occurred. He most certainly did not speak about the history of Palestinian expulsion. And when the pictures of the First Intifada were released—the ones that brought Elkana to speak of the IDF's deeds as barbaric, arguing that the Holocaust must be forgotten—Wiesel remained silent. Apparently, he did not see what it looked like when Jews in uniform act as perpetrators. "In spite of considerable pressure," he once wrote, "I have refused to take a public stand in the Israeli-Arab conflict."[13] One must wonder: Why? Is not silence always on the side of the oppressor? There's no deep wisdom or common sense in Wiesel's silence on Israel. After all, universalist moral critics at least since the Jewish prophets turned their fury also on their own governments and peoples—and indeed primarily on them. Why would a Jewish universalist moral critique refrain from a public stand on Israel?

The answer lies with the collapse of reason through Holocaust messianism. For Mauriac, the relation between "the cross and human suffering" was the "unfathomable mystery" standing at the foundation of faith. The same is true of Wiesel's Holocaust theology. Negating "all answers," lying "outside, if not beyond, history," and defying "knowledge and description,"[14] the Holocaust remains opaque to reason, and stands outside of normal politics—as does the God that was resurrected from this mythical moment. Emerging from this ahistorical, transcendent mystery, Israel remains beyond universalist politics and moral critique. If Wiesel's lifelong Jewish fantasy was to prosecute the dead God like a Job—to bring him to justice for betraying his people at Auschwitz—then his lifelong relation to the living God, the State of Israel, was characterized by the opposite approach. It was akin not to Job's confrontational moral integrity that demanded bringing even the Almighty to justice, but to the dogmatic attitude of Job's friends who put God beyond reason, blindly defending his justice as axiomatic.

To be sure, Wiesel is only an example, but a paradigmatic one. The mythical logic of *mi'shoa le'tkuma* is taught to children in Israeli schools from a young age as the Holocaust's plain meaning, a fact about Israel's existence. It is repeated as a matter of course in official memorial ceremonies, and explained to IDF cadets when they visit Yad Vashem as part of the military's intensive

77

educational programs. "Memory has become a sacred duty of all people of goodwill," Wiesel once told President Obama, and the latter in turn repeated the statement in his preface to the latest edition of Wiesel's *Night*.[15] Perhaps it is a sacred duty. But then only if memory can be disentangled from Holocaust messianism. Only if it can be separated from dangerous political myth.

Elkana, perhaps because he survived Auschwitz as a ten-year-old child, believed such a separation was impossible. And, interestingly enough, he reached this conclusion through an assumption that's not too different from Wiesel's. Consciously or not, he was close to Wiesel's claim that memories of the event defy "knowledge and description." To put it in Jean Améry's terms, Elkana agreed that Holocaust testimonies bring us to the "mind's limit"[16]—but his conclusion was just the opposite of Wiesel's. Precisely because memory in this case brings us to the mind's limits, it *demands* myth. Our main duty, however, is not to memory, but to life, which can only be protected by sane, rational politics. When Primo Levi warned of the "incurable nature of the offence, that spreads like a contagion," he had a similar worry.[17] The "poison of Auschwitz" is flowing together with our "thin blood," he warned, speaking of memory in a way not unlike Nietzsche: it takes away the "strength to begin our lives again."[18] By inviting myth, Holocaust commemoration, according to Elkana, was nothing but such a poison: a threat to civilization, not a shield from barbarism. Memory is therefore anything but a sacred duty. He concluded that the most "important political and educational duty" of Israel's leaders is "to take their stand on the side of life.... They must uproot the domination of that historical *Remember!* over the living."[19]

3.

Israel's current collaboration with the worst type of neofascists and anti-Semitic world leaders makes the threat memory poses to civic politics clear. The list of official state visits by extreme-right politicians to Yad Vashem only in the last few years is alarming. Viktor Orbán, Hungary's nationalist, anti-liberal leader, visited Israel's Holocaust memorial in December, as did Matteo Salvini, the chairman of Italy's neofascist party Lega, who served at the time as his country's deputy prime minister. When Austria's chancellor Sebastian Kurz visited in 2018, his guide took it upon herself to mention that Austria's Freedom Party, with which Kurz is closely allied, was formed by former SS officers. She told the chancellor that some of his current partners should be "informed about what the Holocaust was."[20] The Austrian government officially complained, and the museum issued an apology. *Süddeutsche Zeitung* commented in this context that Yad Vashem was now facing a "difficult decision": Should they take a clear stand on the relation between memory and politics by opposing visits by extreme-right representatives, or let Holocaust commemoration become a "washing machine" for extreme-right, neofascist, and racist politicians?[21]

Unfortunately, even this presentation of the question is too generous to Yad Vashem. The institution has been complicit in whitewashing old extreme right-wing politicians for years. Naftali Bennett, for example, was as Israel's minister of education a frequent guest. As the leader of Israel's religious Zionist settlers' party the New Right, his politics is considerably more violent and racist than that of an Orbán or a Salvini. While in the cabinet, Bennett publicly pronounced: "I killed many Arabs in my life, and there is nothing wrong with that."[22] Shai Piron, Bennett's predecessor as minister of education, is a rabbi who opposes selling houses to Arabs. A reader of the prominent religious blog *Kipa* once turned to Piron's religious advice column, asking whether it was permissible to sell his apartment in Haifa to an Arab family. Piron answered: "Selling the house to an Arab, especially that this violates *Lo Techunem* [*sic*], is forbidden, and selling to Arabs a house especially in light of the current struggle is really strictly forbidden."[23] The Jewish Halacha Lo Techanem forbids the intermingling of Jews with non-Jews, for fear of assimilation. It follows Deuteronomy 7:2, which offers instruction in how the

Israelites, returning from Egypt, should treat the Canaanites who now lived in their land. Some interpreters of Deuteronomy read Lo Techanem as "Give them no quarter"; other interpretations suggest, more plausibly, "Show them no pity." Indeed, the interpretive tradition on which Piron was relying in his answer stipulates that those who are present in Eretz Israel upon the Jews' return should be expelled, enslaved, or even exterminated. During Piron's tenure as education minister, he developed a plan with Yad Vashem to start teaching the history of the Holocaust to Israeli children as early as preschool. Another former education minister is Rafi Peretz, the leader of the religious Zionist list United Right. By any standards, the list represents the extreme right: his allies are Bezalel Smotrich, who supports the expulsions of Palestinians, and Itamar Ben-Gvir. The latter's party, Otzma Yehudit (Jewish Power), is explicitly racist, and was previously forbidden to participate in elections by the Supreme Court: the party has spoken in favor of the massacre of Palestinians and the assassination of Yitzhak Rabin. It is safe to assume that the question of whether Peretz, Bennett, or Piron should be accepted by Yad Vashem has never come up. No official representative of the institution felt the urge to remind these Israeli education ministers "what the Holocaust was." Ben-Gvir, in the meantime, is himself a member of the Knesset.

It may seem obvious that the likes of Peretz, Bennett, or Piron are welcomed by Yad Vashem because they are Jewish and Israeli leaders. There is nothing obvious about this at all. What is obvious is that the racist violence of Israeli politicians advocating policies reminiscent of Nuremberg laws has been normalized by, among other things, Holocaust commemoration, as Elkana feared.

A difficult decision lies ahead for important liberal institutions like the *Süddeutsche Zeitung* or *The New York Times*. Can they recognize the trap such commemoration has become, report the facts, and report the ways in which it has become usual business for Yad Vashem to legitimize the Israeli extreme-right and now, along with them, their natural allies on the European right?

The New York Times reported that Yad Vashem was in a tight spot when it came to Orbán's and Salvini's visits. They had been welcomed by the Israeli government, which provides "40 percent of [the institution's] budget."[24] What goes unsaid here is astonishing in its irresponsibility. Yad Vashem's main private patron was Sheldon Adelson, the right-wing casino mogul who was also the top donor to Donald Trump. Adelson donated to politicians and institutions who promoted his vision of Israel. As mentioned in the introduction, he funded Ariel University's Adelson School of Medicine, in the heart of the West Bank. He was also the owner of the largest circulating and free Israeli daily, *Israel Hayom*, which serves as Netanyahu's main inland propaganda organ. *Makor Rishon*, the settlers' right-wing daily, was another property of

Adelson, edited by Hagai Segal, a terrorist from the Jewish Underground who served time for planting bombs in the cars of Arab politicians. Consider this list: Donald Trump, *Israel Hayom*, Ariel University, *Makor Rishon*, Yad Vashem. Adelson, who passed away early in 2021, knew perfectly well that promoting this type of Holocaust commemoration promoted his kind of politics. When in 2016, against all diplomatic protocol, Netanyahu denounced President Obama's Iran Deal in front of Congress, he said, "The year is 1939, and Iran is Germany."[25] He was accompanied to Capitol Hill by two guests, who sat next to each other to make their presence in the audience known: Sheldon Adelson and Elie Wiesel.

4.

In light of all this, let us remember something else: that for the first thirteen years of Israel's existence, the country took virtually no interest in remembering the Holocaust. If anything, it was a part of history that the young Jewish state preferred to repress. In other words, despite appearances, the relation between Israelis' self-understanding and the Holocaust's memory is not necessary at all.

Invested in developing the image of the new Zionist Jew—

modeled on the image of the heroic pioneer—Israelis had little patience for the survivors' diasporic stories of victimhood. In fact, the systematic extermination of European Jewry was not even regarded an integral part of Jewish history. Ben-Gurion articulated the historiographic principle that guided its exclusion from the nation's chronicles well before the rise of the Third Reich: "The history of a nation is only the history which creates the nation as a single whole," he argued, not that which "happens to individuals and groups within the nation."[26] Still true to this logic, an Israeli textbook on Jewish history published in 1948 devotes a single page to the Holocaust. (The Napoleonic Wars, by comparison, are discussed over ten.)[27] What may now seem axiomatic was back then inconceivable: the Jewish state accepted Jewish survivors and Jewish refugees, but its identity was anything but bound up with their memories. Understood as the survivors' personal story—it happened to *them*, *there*—the Holocaust didn't and couldn't function as a unifying memory, determining Israelis or Jews as a nation. And, certainly, it had nothing to do with Sephardic Jews, who came to Israel from the Muslim countries of the Middle East. As an interruption of a Jewish history and as the antithesis to the Zionist ethos of heroic revival, the Holocaust divided Israelis rather than united them. It was something to be ashamed of, something to be admitted in private rather than memorialized in public.[28]

All this changed abruptly with the capture of Adolf Eichmann in 1960 and, the following year, his prosecution in Jerusalem. Ben-Gurion, in defiance of his earlier understanding of national history, had decided to insert the Holocaust into national memory after all. And not just to insert it, but to assert that this piece of history was the primary unifying principle of Israelis' national identity. Susan Sontag pointed out that the trial was directed like a "work of art"—one of the most "moving and interesting" pieces of art she had seen in years.[29] Indeed Ben-Gurion made no secret of the fact that besides bringing the Nazi criminal to justice he was interested in a form of national theater. As he told the Israeli daily *Yedioth Ahronoth*, "the fate of Eichmann the person has no interest for me at all. What is important is the *spectacle*."[30] The proceedings, accordingly, were not set in a courtroom but on the stage of Beit Ha'Am: the House of the People, a location that was both symbolic and practical. Thousands witnessed the spectacle in the large hall, with survivors seated on stage to testify to the horror of the Holocaust in front of the judges and the nation. Eichmann was also seated on stage, in a glass cage. The proceedings were broadcast live on national radio for those who could not attend.

And a revolution of consciousness was achieved. What was inconceivable before the trial seemed not just obvious, but inevitable, after. The Holocaust now belonged to all Israelis: it was no longer the survivors' personal memory, but everybody's—old Zionist pioneers, young Sabras, and Middle Eastern Jews alike. The new memory rituals—talking about the Holocaust, joining extermination-camp tours, conducting uniformed marches in Yad Vashem and Auschwitz—became sacred duties. Every Passover, Jews reassert that every generation must see itself as if it itself came out of Egypt. Reliving through memory a history of slavery and liberation is a task undertaken by all, as a cornerstone of what it means to be a Jew. After the Eichmann trial, it became natural for Jews to translate Egypt into Germany, and slavery into extermination: *every generation must see itself as if itself came out of Auschwitz*. If before the trial memories of the Holocaust were private memories, by its end they had been nationalized: no longer memories to be ashamed of in silence, but ones to which all of us bear witness together. They make us, the Israelis, who we all are.

And yet whenever such a universal "we" gets asserted, the exclusion of those who are not supposed to belong becomes all the more conspicuous. The Holocaust was presented not as the common concern of all Israeli citizens but of the country's Jewish citizens, and so became a powerful threat to the unifying power of citizenship as such.

To understand this threat, consider the difference between patriotism and nationalism. The terms are often treated as interchangeable, but they are not. Patriotism is primarily a commitment to one's state: it is an old republican virtue, which puts citizenship at the center. A patriot is actively engaged in the political administration and defense of his country and compatriots. The modern politics of nationalism, by contrast, requires a commitment to one's own community and people—a commitment born not of common citizenship, but of common culture, history, and often ethnicity.[31] It is a sad irony that establishing the memory of the Holocaust as the unifying principle for "all" Israelis cemented a nationalist rather than patriotic politics in Israel.

The new unifying principle didn't just exclude Arab Israelis; in fact, it Nazified them, marking them as Hitler's true heirs. En route to a meeting with Angela Merkel in 2015, Netanyahu argued that the Palestinian grand mufti of Jerusalem had convinced Hitler to execute the Final Solution. "Hitler didn't want to exterminate the Jews," Netanyahu explained in his speech, he only "wanted to expel them," but the mufti "protested" that they would all come to Palestine. "What should I do with them?" the Führer allegedly asked.

"Burn them" was the answer, according to Netanyahu, and so Hitler did.[32]

This was a despicable lie, but Netanyahu is hardly alone in telling it. Netanyahu's fairy tale expresses a sentiment for which Ben-Gurion and Yad Vashem are partly responsible as well: during the Eichmann trial, the mufti's alleged role in the Holocaust—and though he certainly was a Hitler sympathizer and met the Führer, he had nothing to do with the Holocaust—was carefully entered into the public testimonies. Similarly, in Yad Vashem's *Encyclopedia of the Holocaust*, the mufti receives a five-page entry. This lengthy discussion is matched only by that of Hitler, who is also allotted five pages. (Goebbels's entry is two pages long. Göring's entry, one.)[33] As Israelis learned to make the Holocaust the basis of national consciousness, it was convenient to think of the Palestinians as proto-Nazis. Allegedly, they fight Zionism not for political causes—land, citizen rights, borders, self-determination, religious sites—but out of a metaphysical, anti-Semitic wish to exterminate the Jews. This in turn legitimizes a certain attitude towards them, and towards those seeking to live with them, collaborate with them politically, and achieve peace. When David Friedman, the US ambassador to Israel, called J Street supporters "worse than kapos,"[34] it was this understanding of the Holocaust he had in mind: the kapos collaborated with their Nazi guards because they had to, in order to survive; liberal two-state supporters are worse, the argument goes, because they collaborate voluntarily with those seeking to exterminate the Jews.

In view of this comment, one wonders what the American ambassador thought at the time of the assassination of Yitzhak Rabin. After Rabin shook Arafat's hand at the White House— striving to end the Intifada and the occupation by finally recog-

nizing the Palestinians' meaningful right to self-determination
—he was marked by many on the right not just as a political rival,
nor even as a mere traitor. In the fierce protests that ensued after
the signing of the Oslo Accord, on the basis of a logic identical to
Friedman's, he was condemned as a Nazi collaborator. Rabin, the
iconic Israeli general, a symbol of the Israeli state if there ever was
any, was portrayed wearing an SS uniform. But it didn't help that
Oslo enjoyed no Jewish majority in Israel, that the agreement was
pushed through the Knesset only with the support of Arab parties
aligned with Rabin's coalition from without. To this clash between
the state and the nation the nation responded aggressively, with
vivid Holocaust imagery. And we know how that ended.[35]

5.

For years, Israelis have taken for granted a muscular politics of
memory; it is time to learn an *ars oblivionalis*—the art, or the
politics, of forgetting. To have a future, Israelis will have to
forget.

The idea is less offensive than it may seem. For one thing, it
should be clear from the above that the Holocaust is being forgotten already, commemoration having become complicit in
abuse. The familiar memory prophets are all too often memory

priests: they proclaim memory to be a sacred duty, an end in itself, only to traffic in it for political gain. The Jewish command *"Zakhor! Remember!"* has been turned into an object of a very un-Jewish idolatry that finds expression in pilgrimages to concentration camps by Israeli high school students, or in flybys over Auschwitz by the Israeli Air Force. The decree *"Remember!"* exists in Judaism, of course, but it is by no means the sole pillar of Jewish culture or faith. The biblical prophets, notably, focused on the moral and political challenges posed by the future. As Yosef Hayim Yerushalmi asks in *Zakhor*, his classic study of Jewish memory, "Is it possible that the antonym of "forgetting" is not 'remembering,' but justice?"—and justice is always about the future.[36] In this light, Renan's injunction to remember to forget could not be more Jewish, while nothing could be less so, less like such a forward-looking, moral cultivation of memory, than the fetishization of the Holocaust. We will not just have a better politics, we will also do better justice to the memory of the Holocaust if we allow ourselves, in this sense, to forget.

6.

"Mr. Speaker, fellow members of Knesset, there is no more natural an occurrence than for the Knesset, of all its factions, to unite and mark International Holocaust Memorial Day": Ahmad Tibi, a longtime Arab Israeli member of the Knesset, opened his speech on January 27, 2010, with what could seem a laconic comment.[37] "This is the place and the time to cry out the cries of all of those who were and are no longer with us, the cries of those who have remained and who are struggling, justifiably so, to unburden themselves from the scenes of death and horror." Most Israelis were deeply moved by these words, but others were enraged. Several members of the Knesset interrupted Tibi from the floor; one had to be sent out by Reuven Rivlin, who was then the house speaker. The speech made that evening's headlines on television, and was reported extensively the next morning in the newspapers.

Arguably, those enraged by the speech understood Tibi better than those who were naively moved by it. Tibi was not speaking as a "good Arab," as Israelis cynically dub Arab Israelis who are almost too sympathetic to Zionist causes. To the contrary. Whereas Israel's parliament represents all Israeli citizens as such, the Holocaust, as we have seen, unites Jews as Jews, and stands as a justification of Arabs' exclusion. Tibi opened his speech stating that there was no "occurrence more natural" than for the Knesset's factions to unite on Holocaust commemoration, and yet he surely knew that for Israel's parliament nothing was less so. Israeli Jews do not assume that Arab Israelis take interest in the Holocaust, nor do they feel they should. Holocaust commemoration is not a joint Arab-Jewish affair by any means. If it was from the ashes of the Holocaust that the Jewish state was born, Arab representatives, whose vocal anti-Zionism is normally tolerated in Israel's parliament, had best commemorate it by, for one, holding their tongues.

Tibi didn't. He meant it when he expressed solidarity with the survivors, but in doing so he revealed a crack in Israelis' commemorations. Exercising his duty to remember with Jews, he asserted his right to live with them, together. And living together can only mean: equally. He refused the idea that he might be excluded by the power of memory.

On first look, it could seem that Tibi's gesture contradicts Elkana's idea that the Holocaust must be, for the sake of democracy, put aside. After all, Elkana claims that there is "no more important political and educational duty" for Israeli leaders to "uproot the domination" of memory from Israeli life. But, in truth—and true to Renan's dictum—by evoking a country where Arabs and Jews remember the Holocaust together Tibi points to a future in which the Holocaust has been, in the best possible sense of the term, forgotten.

Such a politics of forgetting should by no means be confused with an eradication from memory, however. This is clear from the story that Tibi went on to tell—about two survivors, Ovadia Baruch and Aliza Tzarfati, from Thessaloníki:

On March 15, 1943, the first expulsion of the Jews of Thessaloniki was carried out. It was to Auschwitz. The Jews of Thessaloniki, Mr. Speaker, were forced to pay for the train tickets to Auschwitz out of their own pockets.

Ovadia was among them. According to his testimony, it was Dr. Mengele who performed the selection, and he was the only member of his family to be sent to the Auschwitz 1 prison. "When I arrived at the gate, they called me Ovadia Baruch. When I entered the gate, I became 109432."

It was at the camp where he met Aliza. They fell in love. Aliza was then summoned by Dr. Mengele for an experiment. Fortunately for her, there was a Jewish doctor instead, a gynecologist named Dr. Samuel, who was on Mengele's staff. "You are the devil," Aliza screamed at the Jewish doctor. "Alizale, try to stay alive. One day, you'll understand," the doctor said.

In 1945, Ovadia was sent on the death march to the Mauthausen camp. On May 5, 1945, Mauthausen was liberated. Ovadia kept searching and he could not believe that he had found Aliza Tzarfati once again in Greece. It was against all odds. He had asked for her hand in marriage, but she refused because of Mengele's experiments. "We will not have children," Aliza said. He insisted. They were married in 1946.

One day, Aliza told her husband that her stomach had grown. She was pregnant. She had become aware, in retrospect, that the same Dr. Samuel whom she had called "the devil" had intentionally sabotaged Mengele's experiment, and that she was not harmed. The couple would go on to give birth to children. A few weeks after he saved Aliza, Dr. Samuel was caught by the Nazis and executed.

One could choose many types of stories to commemorate the Holocaust's horrors: stories of those who did not survive the death camps or the death marches; stories like Wiesel's, about the sad-eyed angel. Tibi's choice of this one is telling. He celebrates the triumph of those who were saved and reunited, established a home in Israel, and thus bore children. This, you could say, is a Zionist story par excellence, and yet when an Arab Israeli chooses to tell it, it is freed of mythical messianism to become a human story. Tibi, who is a gynecologist, invited Ovadia to join him at the Knesset, to attend the speech as his guest, but Ovadia was hospitalized that day, and could not. What a thought: a Jewish Holocaust survivor coming to Israel's Knesset as the guest of an Arab Israeli representative, on Holocaust Memorial Day. There will be no future for Israel without remembering the Holocaust; but there will be no future for memory without an act of forgetting necessary to denationalize memory and make it a civil affair. Tibi's speech showed that this was not only necessary, but also possible.

"On this day," Tibi continued, one must shed all political identities and "wear one robe only: the robe of humanity." In fact, the humanist power of his speech shines through because he did not speak as a mere human, but as an Arab Israeli representative, by all means aware of his identity. Tibi was fully conscious of years of bloody struggle between Palestinians and Jews, fully aware of the ways in which the Holocaust's memory has been used and abused as a weapon against the people that he represents in the Knesset. But he put his own perspective aside in order to remember with Jews, in solidarity with the people who live with him, as he said "on the same land, in the same country." By remembering to forget, Tibi spoke not merely as a human, but as a neighbor; or better: he spoke as a patriot, but if a patriot then one of a Haifa Republic that still awaits to be created, where Jews and Palestinians speak as equal citizens.

Tibi chose to remain silent on another issue, and this silence may be his most powerful challenge to his Jewish audience. He did not mention the Nakba. This silence contained an invitation. If the establishment of a Jewish state is part of the Holocaust's history—this is a fact that no Israeli would deny—then the history of the Nakba is inseparable from the Holocaust's history, too. Israelis cannot in good faith remember their history of victimhood and redemption—cannot follow the logic of *mi'shoa le'tkuma*—without remembering their role as perpetrators. Since

95

just the opposite is being done, however, Holocaust commemoration has never been truly respected in the Jewish state.

Tibi refrained from mentioning any of this. He took a leap, and remembered to forget the Nakba when speaking of the Holocaust, despite the fact that the Nakba's memory cannot be taken for granted. In this patriotic silence, he demonstrated the willingness to put one's own memories aside, and remember as a citizen. It is now upon us Jews to do the same.

3

Remembering and Forgetting: The Nakba

Doing injustice is worse than suffering it.

—PLATO

1.

ONE DAY LATE IN 1944, soon after the Annual Convention of the Zionist Organization of America came to a close in Atlantic City, Hannah Arendt announced what she thought was a "turning point in Zionist history." The convention had unanimously endorsed a resolution calling for the establishment of a "democratic Jewish commonwealth" in "the whole of Palestine, undivided and undiminished." For Arendt, this was confirmation that the "bitterly repudiated" Revisionist Zionist program—

97

promoting a hard-right nationalist alternative to Ben-Gurion's mainstream-left Zionism—had finally proved "victorious." Unanimous demand for the whole territory implied that after "fifty years of Zionist politics," no genuine difference remained between mainstream Zionists and the Revisionists, whom Jewish intellectuals like Arendt and Albert Einstein denounced as fascists.[1]

The Atlantic City Resolution was especially offensive because it went further than the earlier Biltmore Program (1942), to which Arendt had already objected. In Biltmore, "the Jewish minority" at least granted "minority rights to the Arab majority." In Atlantic City, she wrote, "the Arabs were simply not mentioned." This silence was alarming, Arendt thought: a sign that both mainstream Zionists and Revisionists were now agreed in leaving the Palestinians nothing but "the choice between *voluntary emigration* or second-class citizenship." By "voluntary emigration," she was sarcastically referring to the idea—endorsed in the 1940s by Zionist leadership—that the Palestinians would "voluntarily transfer" out of Palestine. As the author of the essay "We Refugees," Arendt had no doubt that behind such whitewashing words stood a politics of ethnic cleansing.

Seventy-five years later, we can see that Arendt was dead right about the collapse of Zionism into its hard-right Revisionist interpretation. As two-state politics is becoming passé, Israel is de facto claiming the whole of Palestine's territory. Annexations are now the official program of the Likud party; the old-new transfer politics is making a comeback as well.

The idea of transfer accompanied Zionist thinking from its earliest beginnings. Herzl wrote in his diaries that the poor inhabitants of the land taken over for the Jewish state should be "transferred beyond the borders without noise," by denying them work within "our state" and helping to supply it "in transition countries." This "expropriation policy," he added, would have to be carried out "gently and carefully."[2] Israel Zangwill, the prominent British Zionist author, articulated a slogan that reverberated for years, writing that Zionism united "a land without a people" and a "people without a land."[3] This was characteristic hypocrisy. Zangwill was perfectly aware that the land was not without a people, and in his more honest moments he argued that the Jews must be prepared to "drive out by the sword the [Arab] tribes."[4] When Ze'ev Jabotinsky expressed pangs of conscience about the idea of expelling the Palestinians, Zangwill dismissed them as "grandmotherly sentimentalism."[5]

Nevertheless, up until late in Zionist history, transfer fantasies remained fantasies. During World War I, Ben-Gurion wrote, probably in earnest, "We do not intend to push the Arabs aside, to take their land, or to disinherit them."[6] A change of tone came almost instantly after the Peel Commission suggested that Great

Britain partition Palestine, moving Palestinians from some areas designated for Jews. From that moment on, Ben-Gurion's position on transfer—forced, not voluntary—became unequivocal. "The compulsory transfer of the Arabs from the valleys of the proposed Jewish state"—as noted in chapter 2, Ben-Gurion was referring to the Galilee—"could give us something which we never had.... We are being given an opportunity that we never dared to dream of in our wildest imaginings":

> We must grab hold of this conclusion [i.e., recommendation] as we grabbed hold of the Balfour Declaration, even more than that—as we grabbed hold of Zionism itself.... What is inconceivable in normal times is possible in revolutionary times.... Any doubt on our part about the necessity of this transfer, any doubt we cast about the possibility of its implementation, any hesitancy on our part about its justice, may lose [us] an historic opportunity that may not recur.... If we do not succeed in removing the Arabs from our midst, when a royal commission proposes this to England, and transferring them to the Arab area—it will not be achievable easily (and perhaps at all) after the [Jewish] state is established.... This thing must be done now—and the first step—perhaps the crucial [step]—is *conditioning ourselves for its implementation*.[7]

And at the Zionist Congress that followed the Peel Commission, Ben-Gurion asserted,

> In many parts of the land Jewish settlement would not be possible without transferring the Arab peasants. The [Peel] Committee treated seriously this question and it is important that this program came from the Committee and not from us.... We're lucky that the Arab people has immense and empty territories. The growing Jewish power in the land will increase more and more our ability to execute the transfer in large numbers.[8]

In 1944, Moshe Shertok (Sharett), who would become Israel's first foreign minister, said at a meeting of the Jewish Agency, "Transfer can be the crown jewel, the last stage of the political developments, but by no means the starting point. By so doing [talking about transfer too early] you raise tremendous forces against it, and undermine the issue completely.... What will happen when the Jewish state will exist—very likely the result will be a transfer of Arabs."[9] Ben-Gurion spoke at the same meeting: "If I was asked what our plan was, I'd never imagine saying 'transfer.'... This talk can harm in two ways: (a) it can damage international public opinion, because it can create the impression that there's no room [for more Jews] in Eretz Israel without getting the Arabs out...the second damage [is that such an announcement] will put the Arabs...back on their feet."[10] One might say that the doctrine of strategic ambiguity that Israel has adopted with regard to the possession of nuclear weapons—let the Arabs and the world know that we have them, but never condone them officially—was first developed in relation to the Palestinians' expulsion from Palestine. The option was real and there to be seized, provided there was room for Israeli, European, and American deniability.

Strategic ambiguity aside, Ben-Gurion was sure that a Jewish state could not exist amid an Arab majority and that in any case "no people in history" had given up "on its own land of its own goodwill." Thus he endorsed the "forced transfer" of the Palestinians, and argued that there was nothing "immoral about it."[11] When in 1944 Arendt warned that Zionist silence on the Arabs' fate implied the impending cleansing of Palestine, she was not engaging in philosophical speculation: it was a straightforward reading of the political map. And what an earlier generation chose to remain strategically silent about, later generations would prefer to repress.

2.

In mainstream Israeli consciousness, hundreds of thousands of Palestinians miraculously just left their homes once Israel's War of Independence started. Of course, the truth is that no such miracle happened. The Haganah, the paramilitary group from which the IDF was created, implemented its infamous Plan Dalet, which included the command to "capture, cleanse, or destroy" Arab villages, at the discretion of commanders.[12] Officially, Plan Dalet was a military campaign, designed to crush all actual and *potential* Arab hostility within Israel's future borders in preparation for the inevitable war between the tiny state-to-be and its neighboring Arab countries. However, since the Arab population as a whole was viewed as a potential hostile power, the military objective conveniently converged with a demographic one—expelling the Palestinians in order to achieve Jewish ethnic superiority. The result was a systematic attack on Palestinian civilians, accompanied by massive expulsions. Palestinians who did not immediately flee received friendly warnings from top Haganah and IDF leadership that they had better—a whispering campaign that proved extremely effective, not because of Arab cowardice, as Israelis like to believe, but because the whispering was backed by actual massacres.

On April 9, 1948, only a few days after Plan Dalet was beginning to take effect, the Irgun and the Stern Gang—the terrorist branches of the Revisionist Zionist factions—stormed the village of Deir Yassin on Jerusalem's outskirts, backed by Haganah forces. After the village had yielded, its entire population, including women, children, and the elderly, was rounded up; there were killings and rapes. The number of casualties is disputed: estimates range from 100 to 250. All of the survivors were expelled from the territory.[13]

The incident sent shock waves throughout Palestine and the world. Jewish leaders publicly condemned what had happened, and the Jewish Agency issued an apology to the Arab world. Interestingly, Ben-Gurion himself remained silent.[14] Israelis remember this as a singular event: a shameful crime of the Revisionist forces, not the Haganah.

But, in fact, what happened in Deir Yassin was the rule, not the exception, and the hand-wringing that now surrounds the event is a mixture of hypocrisy and repression.

Eleven days after the massacre, with the Arab population still in shock, the battle for Haifa started and soon ended as the city's Palestinian inhabitants departed en masse. The Palestinians in Haifa had numbered seventy thousand: about three thousand remained by the end of the war. Tens of thousands abandoned their homes within forty-eight hours; it was one of the war's and the Nakba's defining moments.

Some of the city's Jewish leaders did urge their Arab neighbors to stay in town, as has been noted by historians,[15] but the attitude of the Haganah leadership was very different. Soldiers received an order to "kill every Arab" they met, and to use firebombs to set on fire "all objectives that can be set on fire."[16] That such policies had been adopted only days after Deir Yassin had everything to do with the flight of Haifa's Palestinians almost overnight, as Israeli leadership would have been well aware.

Indeed they pursued what appears to have been a strategy of provoking mass hysteria. British forces had pledged to protect and evacuate Palestinians who came to the port, and the Arab neighborhoods began to empty out, with people leaving not just their belongings behind but warm meals on the table. According to Zadok Eshel, a combatant in the battle, the Haganah's command, having learned that the Arabs were using loudspeakers to direct evacuees "to gather in the market square," responded by ordering "the commander of the auxiliary weapons company, Ehud Almog,"

> to make use of the three-inch mortars, which were situated next to Rothschild Hospital, and they opened up on the market square where a great crowd [had gathered]. When the shelling started and shells fell into [the crowd], a great panic started. The multitude burst into the port, pushed aside the policemen, stormed the boats and began fleeing the town. Throughout the day the mortars continued to shell the city alternately, and the panic that seized the enemy became a rout.[17]

These bombardments could only have added to the fear of massacre in the aftermath of Deir Yassin, cleansing the city of its

Arabs that much more efficiently.[18] British testimony further records that "during the morning,"

> [the Haganah] were continually shooting down on all Arabs who moved, both in Wadi Nisnas and the Old City. This included completely indiscriminate and revolving machine-gun fire and sniping on women and children ... attempting to get out of Haifa through the gates into the docks.... There was considerable congestion outside the [port's] East Gate of hysterical and terrified Arab women and children and old people on whom the Jews opened up mercilessly with fire.[19]

Golda Meir (then still Meirson) toured Haifa shortly after this. She wrote,

> It is a dreadful thing to see the dead city. Next to the port I found children, the old, waiting for a way to leave. I entered the houses, there were houses where the coffee and pita bread were left on the table, and I could not avoid [thinking] that this, indeed had been the picture in many Jewish towns [during World War II, in Europe].[20]

Details vary, but a similar fate awaited the Palestinian inhabitants of every other city in the new state, Arab or mixed: Jerusalem,

Jaffa, Tiberias, Ashdod, al-Majdal (Ashkelon), Beersheba, Tsfat, Lydda, and Ramleh. The case of the latter two is noteworthy, because Ben-Gurion himself happened to be present on the scene, and, according to field commanders' reports, is said to have issued a command to expel the Palestinians. Not in writing, but then, it was at Lydda and Ramleh that the one written order of expulsion was delivered, signed by top Haganah leadership: "1. Expel quickly the inhabitants of Lydda without distinguishing their ages. Direct them to Beit Nabala. 2. Execute immediately."[21] The order was given by two young officers: Yigal Allon, Israel's future foreign minister, and Yitzhak Rabin, who was the one to sign it.

The fate of smaller villages was often akin to that of Deir Yassin. An entry in the diary of Yosef Nahmani, a Haganah commander who participated in the cleansing of the Galilee, gives a taste of the methods that led hundreds of thousands of Arabs to flee:

[In Safsaf, after] the inhabitants raised a white flag, they assembled the men and women separately, bound the hands of fifty or sixty villagers, shot and killed them, and buried them in a single pit. They also raped several of the village women. Near the thicket, he … saw several dead women, among them a woman clutching her dead child. In Eilabun and Faradia, they greeted the soldiers with white flags…. [The soldiers] opened fire and after thirty people had been killed they started moving the rest on foot... [towards] Lebanon. In Salha, which raised the white flag, there was a real massacre. They killed men and women, about sixty to seventy. Where did they learn such a cruel conduct such as that of the Nazis?... One officer told me that the most eager were those who had come from the camps.[22]

3.

Israeli society has never confronted this history. We were taught to ask our parents and grandparents about their experiences in the Holocaust and to perceive the Jews as victims—which we surely were—but never as perpetrators, which we also were. In fact, Yad Vashem, with its exhortation to "never forget," overlooks the village of Deir Yassin, and not from too far away. But the occasion to ask about the Nakba has hardly ever been there. The remains of hundreds of abandoned Arab villages were bulldozed or detonated immediately after the war: the destruction was aimed to execute what has been called "retroactive transfer"—preventing the refugees' return—but also served to eliminate the facts and eradicate memories. Few Israelis know that some 350 Arab villages were abandoned and destroyed; that the campus of Tel Aviv University is built on the rubble of an destroyed village, Al-Shaykh Muwannis; or that cities such as Ashkelon, Ashdod, or Beersheba, today prosperous Jewish cities, were Arab towns until 1948. The documents that testify to the government's policies remain heavily censored to date. We do, for all that, know that Yosef Weitz, a high official in the Jewish National Fund, was a chairman of the Transfer Committee appointed by the government to devise policies for the prevention of the refugees' return and systematic plans for the removal of those Arabs who did not leave.[23] Weitz, one of the earliest and most ardent transfer advocates, articulated his vision already in 1940, insisting, as Ben-Gurion did not, on a complete transfer of the Arab population, not just one sufficient to ensure a Jewish majority:

> Among ourselves it must be clear that there is no room in the country for both peoples.... If the Arabs leave it, the country will become wide and spacious for us.... The only solution [after World War II ends] is a Land of Israel, at least a western Land of Israel, without Arabs. There is no room here for compromises.... There is no way but to transfer the Arabs from here to the neighboring countries, to transfer all of them, apart perhaps from [the predominantly Christian] Bethlehem, Nazareth, and old Jerusalem. Not one village must be left, not one tribe. The transfer must be directed at Iraq, Syria, and even Transjordan. For this goal, funds will be found.... And only after this transfer will the country be able to absorb millions of our brothers and

the Jewish problem [in Europe] will cease to exist. There is no other solution.[24]

The evidence that there was a will to expel the Arabs, that a way was found to do it, and that it was done is unarguable, and yet in Israel strategic ambiguity has continued to veil it in doubt. There can be no doubt. We have Weitz. We have Moshe Dayan, in 1950 remarking that Israel must regard the Arabs "who remained in the country as if their destiny hasn't yet been settled. I hope that in the next years there will be *another* possibility to carry out a transfer of these Arabs from Israel" (my emphasis).[25] This makes it clear what Israel's iconic war strategist thought that he was up to as a Haganah and IDF commander only two years before. In all likelihood, if the military censor had noticed that word, it would be erased with a black marker. Memory is said to be the sacred duty in the Jewish state, but only where the Holocaust is concerned. When the Nakba is at stake, the duty is to deny, censor, and forget.[26]

4.

Israeli intellectuals on the left and American liberal Zionist authors have been for the most part complicit in this situation.

Authors such as Amos Oz or David Grossman—or, in the United States, Michael Walzer—have focused on the occupation as Israel's original sin, an accident that happened to the Jewish state in 1967 and must be fixed in order to return to Ben-Gurion's just, left-Zionist idea. Admitting that a Jewish state is politically and historically inseparable from the achievement of Jewish demographic superiority is to admit that the idea was hardly originally just and that this politics is not the place to return to. By the same token, there is no understanding of the occupation, its logic, politics, and reasons—if these authors wanted to understand it— without understanding the Nakba.

Jamal Zahalka, an Arab Israeli lawmaker, once accused Israel's Zionist left of racist hypocrisy from the Knesset podium. Ben-Gurion's labor party, he pointed out, had been responsible for the Nakba, while the Israeli right was at least honest about its racist politics. Subsequently, a curt letter appeared in *Haaretz*. It reads:

I actually understand well why PM Jamal Zahalka hates the Israeli left and prefers the right.... If not for the Israeli left in 1948, with its kibbutzim and moshavim, the Haganah and the Palmach, the Palestinians would have had no Nakba. No Palestinian would have lost his home. On the contrary: the Palestinians would have taken over a quarter of a million Jewish homes.
—Amos Oz, Tel Aviv, September 11, 2015

To the best of my knowledge, this characteristically condescending remark is all that Israel's leading public intellectual of the last fifty years has ever found to say about the obliteration of a whole society and culture. Predictably, the Palestinians are blamed for their own plight. Israeli responsibility is depicted, true to the common myth, as necessary self-defense. Nothing is said about the necessity of establishing Jewish demographic superiority.

This failure is especially striking because Israeli authors who were active before 1948 and witnessed the war did not keep silent. S. Yizhar's 1949 *Khirbet Khizeh*—as well as his 1958 *The Days of Ziklag*, widely regarded as Israel's defining War of Independence epic—contain excruciating descriptions of Israeli war crimes. In stories that are told from a reflective first-person perspective, and not from that of the Zionist collective (Yizhar's prose was groundbreaking in Hebrew in this regard) he does not shy away from employing Holocaust imagery in his descriptions of the Nakba, deliberately blending in his protagonists' and thus readers' minds the Holocaust's victims and the Nakba's perpetrators. The writers of the following generation would be much more ideologically defined; at times, their attitude bordered on that of party intellectuals.

In 1961, Oz, along with Muki Tsur, Amnon Barzel, and other promising young writers from the kibbutz movement, set up two meetings with Ben-Gurion, asking to warn the prime minister about some dangerous literary developments.[27] "I'll send you a book by [Yehuda] Amichai," said Barzel to Ben-Gurion, as reported in the conversation's transcripts found in the Ben-Gurion Archives. "He is an excellent poet, but extremely dangerous":

TSUR: "The fact is that [Amichai's words] represent something one has to resist.... And you, for reasons that I do not want to dwell upon—the fact that you ignore it, is dangerous."

"Amichai represents nihilism?" [Ben-Gurion] asked....
TSUR: "Of course."
BEN-GURION: "I can't stand nihilism."...

...

BEN-GURION [TO OZ]: "Do you place [Amichai] together with Yizhar?"

...

OZ: "There is a certain similarity [to Yizhar] as a writer, not as a person."
BEN-GURION: "Are you referring to *Yemei Ziklag* [Yizhar's monumental war novel, *Days of Ziklag*]?"
OZ: "Especially to *Days of Ziklag*."

When Ben-Gurion and the young literati worried about "nihilism," they were not thinking about philosophical questions. These authors were "dangerous" because their work gave rise to an *uncertainty about the Zionist way*. Their writings were "nihilist" because they were moral rather than ideological: they conveyed painful doubts about meaning and purpose—heightened by memories of the crimes of the Nakba—when meaning and purpose should have been settled by Zionist ideology. It is this lasting attachment to the official Zionist party line that would make an Amos Oz a harsh critic of the occupation, which he alleged had corrupted Zionism. For the same reason, he was no less an opponent of recognizing the Nakba as integral to Israeli consciousness.

At one point in his conversation with the young writers, Ben-Gurion suddenly turned directly to Oz: "Your conclusion, Amos, is one: a dictatorship. Yes, yes."

"Heaven forbid," Oz immediately answered. Clearly, however, Ben-Gurion was responding to ideas about censorship, which had been suggested.

"Can you silence Amichai?" Ben-Gurion asked rhetorically.

"What do you think can be done?" asked another kibbutznik.

Ben-Gurion answered: "Dictatorship could be a solution. To force people. This solution does not suit us because you are dealing with Jews...you cannot have a dictatorship over them."

Censorship can be as subtle as it is forcible, and this discussion with Ben-Gurion about what was not to be said about the Nakba bears on how the story of the Six-Day War came to be told, very much with Oz's contriving. In 1967, only days after the war's end, Oz, Avraham Shapira, Muki Tsur, and others recorded a series of conversations with soldiers who had just returned from the front. These were quickly transcribed and published as a book under the title *Warriors' Conversations*.[28] The book was a sensation. The returning young soldiers were depicted not merely as war heroes, but as deeply reflective and morally self-questioning people who were wholly engaged with the nation's craving for peace. The book thus demonstrated the triumph of Zionist education: Israel was superior not only as a military power, but also as a moral force, a sentiment that was captured by a cliché the book served to popularize: *yorim ve'bochim*, shooting while crying. Golda Meir regarded *Warriors' Conversations* as a "holy book"; Haim Gouri suggested that it molded "the soul and consciousness of an entire generation." [29] Everybody today is familiar with the idea that Israeli soldiers keep "the purity of arms" and the slogan that the IDF is "the most moral military in the world."

Recently, thanks to the documentary *Censored Voices* (2015), it has become clear what a production—indeed, construction—*Warriors' Conversations* was. *Censored Voices* is composed from material that was cut from the book. In it we hear Oz speaking of the "euphoria" that swept Israel after the war, but also of other sentiments, including deep moral anxieties that troubled soldiers who returned from the war. Giving these anxieties voice, he says, may not "contribute much to what people call 'national morale,'" but then, he adds, the point of the project is different: "We will make a small contribution to the truth."[30]

They did the exact opposite, however. As Tom Segev, following Alon Gan, has shown, the conversations were heavily censored—and, at times, flatly rewritten—not just by the military censor, whose intervention was surprisingly limited, but mostly by the editors themselves. They omitted remarks that questioned the war's cause, and, in general, anything that got in the way of the national morale and the Zionist story. They also made sure to cut out all talk of expulsions of villagers or war crimes. One speaker was quoted in *Warriors' Conversations* as saying about the war, "Some very negative things [have been] revealed." What he is recorded as saying is: "Some very negative things are revealed when you see soldiers shooting at defenseless civilians . . . elderly people." A soldier recorded as saying his unit had been ordered to "kill" anyone who crossed the Jordan River was quoted in the book as saying only that he was ordered to "prevent" the crossing. Another soldier speaks of his troop encountering a wounded enemy soldier on the side of the road and debating whether to kill him; then, out of the blue, one of them shot the wounded soldier in the head. How does *Warriors' Conversations* report this? "One guy suggested killing him. Of course, we wouldn't allow it." Another IDF soldier recalls that attacking civilians made him feel like "a member of the Gestapo," and some kibbutzniks mention feeling like SS soldiers when they obeyed orders to expel entire Palestinian villages. None of this was published.[31] These are representative samples of the systematic censorship or alteration of information that was done to produce the kind of book that Golda Meir would consider "holy."

And *Censored Voices* is still invested in the myth it investigates. It opens with the statement that the IDF "censored the recordings, allowing the kibbutzniks to publish only 30 percent of the conversations." But, again, the military actually interfered very little: most of the censorship was performed by Israel's emerging left-Zionist intellectuals, a fact that *Censored Voices* does not take into account at all. Oz is celebrated on screen as an anti-occupation intellectual hero, but never confronted with the fact that he participated in producing a falsified document. And he is never asked a single question about what guided the editors' work: how they decided what to print and what to cut or rewrite altogether.

We can turn to Oz and Tsur's earlier conversations with Ben-Gurion for answers. An uncensored *Warriors' Conversations* would have presented Israelis' deep doubts about the Zionist way—a feeling of a lost purpose, brought on by participating in war crimes comparable and continuous to those of the Nakba. An authentic *Warriors' Conversations* would have been too close to the so-called "nihilism" of Amichai's poetry and Yizhar's *Khirbet Khizeh* and *The Days of Ziklag*. And this would not do. Asked at the end of *Censored Voices* what he feels when he listens to the censored recordings, Oz replies: "I feel that we spoke the truth, a truth that I stand by to this day."

5.

The liberal intellectual narrative and the suppression of the Nakba that accompanies it is beginning, however, to face challenges. Ari Shavit's 2013 *My Promised Land: The Triumph and Tragedy of Israel*, for example, does break a certain amount of new ground.[32] A major best seller in North America, the book was celebrated as a conversation changer: *The New Yorker* excerpted it; and *The New York Times* ran three glowing reviews.[33] Shavit's main thesis is that the occupation—deplorable and pernicious as it may be—isn't Israel's main problem. The country has deeper historical and existential reckonings to make. First, the historical fact of the expulsion of the Palestinians must be openly admitted. Second, it is necessary to recognize that the demographic problem that led to this expulsion continues to be the main threat to Israel's existence. "Today 46 percent of all of the inhabitants of greater Israel are Palestinians," Shavit writes. "Their share of the overall population is expected to rise to 50 percent by 2020 and 55 percent by 2040. If present trends persist, the future of Zion will be non-Zionist."[34] Lastly, Shavit warns of the danger of being "blinded by political correctness."[35] The Tel Aviv elite, he argues, "instilled *ad absurdum* a rigid political correctness by turning the constructive means of self-criticism into an obsessive deconstructive end of its own"[36]—that is, through excessive self-criticism, Israel has lost its national unity and sense of justification. Americans and Europeans can perhaps afford the luxury of being "politically correct" about things, Shavit contends, but Israelis cannot: only by the sword can Jews survive in the Middle East. They have no choice but to get their hands dirty.

Shavit, in short, is a liberal Zionist who recognizes the Nakba's role in Israel's national narrative, and this is no mean achievement. We see this most clearly in the book's Lydda chapter—the one that gave it its fame—in which Shavit retells the city's story of expulsion and massacres:

By evening, tens of thousands of Palestinian Arabs leave Lydda in a long column . . . disappearing into the East. Zionism obliterates the city of Lydda.

Lydda is our black box. In it lies the dark secret of Zionism. The truth is that Zionism could not bear Lydda. From the very beginning there was a substantial contradiction between Zionism and Lydda. If Zionism was to be, Lydda could not be.... Lydda was an obstacle blocking the road to the Jewish state and ... one day Zionism would have to remove it.[37]

In describing Lydda as Zionism's "black box" and "dark secret," in recognizing that "substantial contradiction," Shavit accomplished something that Israeli liberal intellectuals like Oz et al. had refused to even attempt.

The acknowledgment, however, only goes so far: throughout his book, for example, Shavit carefully avoids even using the word "Nakba." In such a book, this cannot be an accident but rather a conscious decision: the refusal to name the occurence is a refusal to recognize it as history. As we continue reading this "least tendentious book" about Israel, as Leon Wieseltier described it, we discover that not mentioning the Nakba is in line with Shavit's later argument, which is to concede the expulsions and massacres happened and to embrace that hard truth for the sake of Israel. Thus, he writes, "if need be, I'll stand by the damned"—referring to those Israeli war criminals who are responsible to Lydda. "If it wasn't for them," he explains, "the State of Israel would not have been born.... They did the dirty, filthy work that enables my people, myself, my daughter, and my sons to live."[38]

Despite appearances, this isn't a courageous confession of

Israel's existential tragedy. On the contrary: such statements are designed to disarm the tragedy's impact on Israeli consciousness—dismissing its relevance to current Israeli concerns or the future of liberal Zionism. To think otherwise, we are told, is to yield to political correctness. Far from incorporating the Nakba into liberal Zionist consciousness, Shavit transforms that into the consciousness of the right, which has never had any need to repress the facts.

The left's relation to memory and tragedy is relatively easy to distinguish from that of the right. Being on the left consists in the understanding that a people must change, sometimes radically, in order to come to terms with the tragic past. By contrast, being on the right consists in endorsing your people's history and tragedy as givens—embracing them as the inescapable preconditions of who you are. Under a pretense of liberalism, Shavit does just that. "The choice is stark," Shavit concludes: "either reject Zionism because of Lydda, or accept Zionism along with Lydda."[39] Somehow, the one reasonable possibility remains unmentioned: that Zionism need not be rejected because of Lydda, nor ever, absolutely never, accepted along with it; that confronting Lydda, and Haifa, and Deir Yassin, and Safsaf—and so many other names of places in our country and our past—means that Zionism must be *transformed*.

Susie Linfield, in an interview she conducted with Shavit, gets to the root of his confusion. Shavit is "essentially arguing,"

Linfield points out, "that war crimes can be committed even in the course of a just war." The war's justness "is not erased by such crimes; conversely, the criminality—the barbarism—of the acts in question cannot be mitigated by the justness of the cause."[40] That's how Shavit would like his argument to be seen, but we must ask what he considers to be a just war. For Shavit the Nakba is about Israel's survival, but this is misleading—misleading in the same way that not mentioning the Palestinians in the 1944 Atlantic City Resolution was. As Arendt knew then, what's at stake isn't *bare* survival, but ensuring the ethnic Jewish majority that's necessary for a Jewish democracy. In other words, and Shavit *is* clear that this is Zionism's "dark secret," the violent mass expulsions of Palestinians did not just happen in the course of the war. They were intrinsic to the war's aims, yet still he deems them just. Hopefully the future's liberal Zionists will look at this reasoning and refuse to budge: if you're willing to accept ethnic cleansing as a just cause, no doubt you will end up thinking that your war's "justness" isn't diminished by war crimes committed in its midst. Logically, this is consistent, but this is the logic of the right—the violent far right even—rather than of what anyone would recognize as the left.

But Shavit will have none of it: that is all "political correctness," or what Zangwill, a hundred years earlier, dismissed as "grand-motherly sentimentalism." With the demise of the two-state solution, the "dirty, filthy" work Shavit justifies as a necessary part of Israel's past may now be invoked as necessary to secure its future. The chauvinist willingness to dismiss human conscience as grandmotherly sentimentalism threatens to degrade Zionist politics into a form of barbarism.

6.

For years, transfer politics has remained more or less dormant in Israel, not because violent ethnic politics had been entirely delegitimized but because it had been successfully executed. In 1947, 600,000 Jews lived in Palestine in the midst of 1.2 million Palestinians. In 1948, by the end of the war, approximately 500,000 Palestinians remained, and soon waves of Jewish immigrants began to arrive. Jews comprised 77 percent of Israel's voting population in the last elections, but this figure is misleading, since they constitute barely 50 percent of the population within the borders in which they vote. As a consequence, the long-repressed politics of transfer is making a return—with a vengeance.

In the April 2019 elections, two parties were known as explicit advocates of transfer. The first was Avigdor Lieberman's Israel Our Home, whose 2014 platform had included the idea that Arabs "from Jaffa or Acre," that is, Israeli citizens, suffering as they do from the problem of "split identity," should be offered money and assistance to emigrate.[41] Israel's former defense and foreign minister, in other words, was promoting the old idea of "voluntary transfer." Often considered a pragmatist, Lieberman is an openly racist politician who has publicly called for a Jewish boycott on Arab businesses. Is it mere speculation to suppose this "pragmatist" would not be averse also to less "civilized" methods of expulsion?

Tkuma, running under the United Right, was more outspoken yet. In September 2017, the party officially incorporated into its platform Bezalel Smotrich's so-called Triumph Plan, calling for the annexation of the West Bank and presenting the Palestinians with a threefold choice. The first is to accept apartheid: to abandon any "national ambitions," declare loyalty to the Jewish state, and be allowed to remain in its territory with resident, but not citizen, status. The second is voluntary transfer: Israel would provide financial and diplomatic assistance to resettle in a neighboring Arab country. The third option, for those who choose to stay, but not on the proffered terms, is "being taken care of by the IDF."[42] Without a doubt, most Palestinians would choose to stay on their own terms. When Smotrich, who was back then Israel's minister of transportation and a member of Cabinet, was asked how the IDF would take care of families, women, and children, he answered, "as in war."[43] His plan, he added, was based on the example of Joshua in the Bible, where non-Jews living in the Holy Land indeed receive a threefold option: bow to Jewish rule, leave the land, or be killed.

Netanyahu addressed the Tkuma party convention, in which this Triumph Plan was discussed and approved, by video: "I was delighted to hear that you dedicate the discussions to the question of the future of Eretz Israel," the prime minister said on the screen. Alluding to Zangwill's original slogan that Zionism married "a people without a land" to a land "without a people," he added, "Until recently, this land was empty and forsaken. But since we returned to Zion, after years of exile, it is blooming again."[44] Netanyahu is very well acquainted with Zangwill and the idea of transfer. His father, the Revisionist historian Ben-Zion Netanyahu, was the editor of a volume of Zangwill's speeches and a transfer enthusiast who lamented that there had been no occasion to move the Palestinians in the turmoil of World War I.[45] Jabotinsky opposed transfer throughout his life, but just before his death he was "converted" after meeting Ben-Zion Netanyahu.[46] Under Benjamin Netanyahu's blessing, the United Right also brought Jewish Power under its umbrella; this was an explicitly racist party previously banned from participating in elections by the Supreme Court. Not only does the United Right support the forced transfer of all Arabs, it also spoke in favor of the assassination of Rabin, and, after Ariel Sharon promoted the evacuation of settlers from Gaza, celebrated his stroke. In the March 2019 elections, thanks to Netanyahu's repeated efforts, its representative, Itamar Ben-Gvir, finally managed to get into the Knesset.

The Likud party now officially endorses the annexation of the West Bank, and in the current atmosphere, annexation has begun to figure as an almost moderate-sounding alternative to transfer. Taking over the West Bank implies taking some thought about the situation of its 3 million Palestinian inhabitants. Officially, Likud representatives have proposed "apartheid with a human face": letting Palestinians live under Israeli law rather than the military law of the occupation, but without granting them citizenship status. This presupposes that the Palestinians would find such arrangements acceptable, and they would not. What will these moderate annexationists do when half the West Bank's population violently resists being stripped of national and human rights? How will they, as they will certainly present the case, defend Israel?

7.

In *My Promised Land* Shavit carefully avoids saying anything meaningful about the future, a political correctness of his own, you might say. Demography was the politics of the past, and is the politics of the future, too. Put into practice, Shavit's romantic Zionist principles—so warmly embraced by liberals in North America—are indistinguishable from the politics of transfer.

Back in 2004, Shavit interviewed Benny Morris, Israel's greatest expert on the expulsion of the Palestinians, for *Haaretz*.[47] The conversation is worth revisiting. Clearly, it inspired Shavit to write his best-selling book about Zionism's "dark secret." It also makes clear that Shavit knew that the deeper, darker secret concerns Israel's future rather than its past:

Ben-Gurion was a "transferist"?

"Of course. Ben-Gurion was a transferist. He understood that there could be no Jewish state with a large and hostile Arab minority in its midst. . . ."

I don't hear you condemning him.

"Ben-Gurion was right. If he had not done what he did, a state would not have come into being. That has to be clear. . . . Without uprooting the Palestinians, a Jewish state would not have arisen here."

. . . In the end, do you in effect justify all this? Are you an advocate of the transfer of 1948?

"There is no justification of rape. There is no justification of acts of massacre. Those are war crimes. But in certain conditions, expulsion is not a war crime. I don't think that the expulsions of 1948 were war crimes. You can't make an omelet without breaking eggs. You have to dirty your hands."

. . .

So when the commanders of Operation Dani are standing there and observing the long and terrible column of 50,000 people expelled from [Lydda] walking eastward, you stand there with them? You justify them?

"I definitely understand them.... I don't think they felt any pangs of conscience, and in their place, I wouldn't have felt pangs of conscience."

You do not condemn them morally?

"No."

They perpetrated ethnic cleansing.

"There are circumstances in history that justify ethnic cleansing...."

. . .

"From my point of view, the need to establish this state in this place overcame the injustice that was done to the Palestinians by uprooting them."

And morally speaking, you have no problem with that deed?

"That is correct. Even the great American democracy could not have been created without the annihilation of the Indians. There are cases in which the overall, final good justifies harsh and cruel acts that are committed in the course of history."

And in our case it effectively justifies population transfer.

"That's what emerges.

...

I think [Ben-Gurion] made a serious historical mistake in 1948. Even though he understood the demographic issue and the need to establish a Jewish state without a large Arab minority, he got cold feet during the war. In the end, he faltered."

I'm not sure I understand. Are you saying that Ben-Gurion erred in expelling too few Arabs?

"If he was already engaged in expulsion, maybe he should have done a complete job. I know that this stuns the Arabs and the *liberals and the politically correct* types [my emphasis]. But my feeling is that this place would be quieter and know less suffering if the matter had been resolved once and for all, if Ben-Gurion had carried out a large expulsion and cleansed the whole country—the whole Land of Israel, as far as the Jordan River. It may yet turn out that this was his fatal mistake. If he had carried out a full expulsion—rather than a partial one—he would have stabilized the State of Israel for generations."

...

And today? Do you advocate a transfer today?

"If you are asking me whether I support the transfer and expulsion of the Arabs from the West Bank, Gaza and perhaps even from the Galilee and the Triangle, I say not at this moment.

I am not willing to be a partner to that act. *In the present circumstances*, it is neither moral nor realistic."

Here Morris aligns himself not with Ben-Gurion, but with Yosef Weitz. Shavit's *My Promised Land* is close to Morris's position, but equivocal about the question of complete transfer as it is about the relation of the past to the future. He never addresses in his own book the question, the truly burning question, that he had posed to Morris: Did Ben-Gurion err by not doing a complete job? And, since the job was not complete, should it be completed in the future?

8.

In 1989, at a Peace Now rally, Amos Oz harshly denounced Israel's extreme right, then still on the delegitimized margin, for entertaining "the idea of expelling and driving out the Arabs, deceitfully called here 'transfer'...we must rise and say simply and sharply: It is an impossible idea. We will not let you expel the Arabs." And, he continued, "Israel's right must know that there are acts that, if attempted, will cause the split of the state."[48]

This is a bold moral statement, but we have seen that it is based on a hypocritical misunderstanding of Israeli history. Just as

Arendt foresaw in 1944, and later Zionist intellectuals preferred to forget, ethnic cleansing is not an "impossible idea." Israel executed it in the past, with an alarming degree of success. Now in our post-two-state era, the question of ethnic cleansing is once again alive, and liberal Zionists are confronted with two political options. Will they support an ethnic Jewish nationalism that rules over a majority Arab population, a nationalism for which a politics not merely of annexation and apartheid but of transfer is a given, or will they embrace the alternative? The nature of that alternative is clear enough. It means acknowledging the Nakba, the better to engage in a genuinely democratic, Arab-Jewish collaboration, based on fully equal citizenship. This does *not* require abandoning a program of Zionist national self-determination, but it does require a transformation of Zionism into something greater than a commitment to a Jewish state. That transformation begins a change of consciousness: a decision to choose a common life, and common citizenship, with the Palestinian people born of a real recognition of the "dark secret" of Israel's history. That's the only alternative to repressing and repeating our crimes. A dialectical politics of memory and forgetting of the Nakba as much as the Holocaust will have to be embraced.

In an essay titled "Your Holocaust, Our Nakba," the late Emile Habibi, an Arab Israeli author and member of the Knesset, commented on the intertwining of the two:

I cannot imagine that, had the Holocaust not happened, the brothers of Heinrich Heine and Maimonides, Bertolt Brecht and Stefan Zweig, Albert Einstein and the immortal Arab-Jewish poet Shlomo Ben Ovadia would have permitted a Jewish government to expel another Semite people out of its home.... Indeed, the horrifying suffering inflicted on the Jews by the Nazi beast can be measured not only by the six million annihilated in the concentration camps and by other means of mass killings. It is measured also by the terrible price the Jewish people have paid in losing their glorious Jewish tradition and in the damage it has caused to what is called the "Jewish heart."[49]

It is interesting to compare Habibi's words to Ahmad Tibi's Holocaust Memorial Day speech. When speaking about the Holocaust, Tibi refrained from mentioning the Nakba, demonstrating that it is possible to put one's own memories aside in order to remember as a citizen, in solidarity with his compatriots' history. He did not remind Israelis of the inherent relation between the Holocaust and the Nakba—say, of the fact that Holocaust survivors participated in the expulsion of his people, or that European Jewish refugees were permanently settled in the abandoned homes of Palestinians who had become refugees themselves. Both the Holocaust and the Nakba are central to Israel's fraught past. Its future depends, as Renan knew, on a politics of common acknowledgment and forgetting. The Jewish leaders of an Arab-Jewish alliance would have to insist that their country must finally take responsibility for the Nakba's crime: investigate it, teach it, commemorate it, and insist that expulsion is a crime that ought never be repeated, precisely because it could happen again. So far, however, neither Israel's public intellectuals nor its left-liberal leaders have found the courage to rise to this challenge. Not a single Nakba speech comparable to Tibi's Holocaust Memorial gesture has been delivered in the Knesset. Such a gesture would hardly be an exercise in correctness: for there to be common citizenship Jews and Palestinians must have a history in common. And if we do, one day, then our Palestinian compatriots could be expected to forget.

4

The Haifa Republic

The crisis consists precisely in the fact that the old is dying and
the new cannot be born.

—Antonio Gramsci

1.

In September 2015, Mahmoud Abbas announced to the
Assembly of the United Nations that the Palestinians would no
longer "continue to be bound" by the Oslo Agreements. He had
warned in advance that he was going to drop a "bombshell," but
given that the Oslo process had already been irrelevant for several
years, the significance of this announcement was difficult to make
out. *The New York Times* reported on this speech with a headline
and went on to dismiss the pronouncement as "old, old, old, old

news."[1] *Haaretz*'s report was no less anticlimactic, writing that even if Abbas had "dropped a bombshell," nothing seemed to have actually been "detonated."[2]

And yet Abbas's statement was, in its way, monumental. For a long time everybody had known that Oslo was dead, and yet everybody was still looking the other way, keeping the comfortable Oslo Illusion alive. "Oslo" had become a code name for maintaining the status quo, while "maintaining the status quo" was only a coded way of accepting the irreversible development of Israel's occupation project. George Orwell is claimed to have said that "at times of universal deceit speaking the truth is a revolutionary act," and Abbas's announcement was a refusal to condone the fictions of the powers that be—not that what a Palestinian leader had to say, however, was really thought to matter.

No, it took Donald Trump's election as president of the United States for people to finally abandon the Oslo Illusion. A bullshit artist cares so little about the truth that, unlike more sincere world leaders, he may forget to lie. Asked about the two-state solution at a press conference immediately after assuming office, Trump, standing next to Netanyahu, replied, "I am looking at two-state, and one-state, and I like the one that both parties like."[3] Basically, the American president said "Whatever," and Netanyahu, undoubtedly astonished at hearing America's decades-long commitment to territorial compromise dismissed offhand, began to giggle loudly in the background.[4] In any case, Trump was being far more truthful than Obama, Kerry, Clinton, and Merkel, et al., had been in years gone by, as they laconically intoned that "soon, the window of opportunity for the two-state solution would close." Similarly, Trump's announcement in May 2018 that the US embassy would move to Jerusalem, and his recognition at the same time of Israel's annexation of the Golan Heights, made no real difference to how things stood in fact—and yet his actions dealt a blow to the prevalent bad faith.[5] Oslo is now over once and for all, and though the danger of the moment is greater than ever, this is also a moment of opportunity. The truth is out: There will be no two-state solution. There could, however, still be a worthwhile one-state alternative, and it is time to start the fight for it.

In the 1990s, the Oslo Agreement was not the Oslo Illusion: it made the two-state dream a concrete political possibility. Of course, it was heavily criticized from both right and left, for reasons good and bad. The Palestinians, who had been a majority in Mandate Palestine, were expected to give up all claims to the lands from which they had been expelled and to permanently settle on 22 percent of the territory—a massive concession to make. The Israelis, for their part, would have had to evacuate thousands of settlers—something that threatened to tear apart

Israeli society—in the belief that by doing so, Palestinian terror-
ism would end and Arab recognition of Israel's right to exist
would follow. There was immense skepticism, and yet virtually
everyone who wanted peace, including ideological one-state supporters, found Oslo to be an acceptable compromise.[6] Indeed, a
compromise is exactly what it was: ideology and justice aside,
there had never been a comparably ambitious or substantial peace
plan in the history of the Israeli-Palestinian conflict. In some
circles on the left, it is now customary to doubt whether Oslo
was ever intended seriously, but it seemed serious enough at the
time to lead to the assassination of an Israeli prime minister.
Yitzhak Rabin, and Yigal Amir, his murderer, knew that what
was at stake was no illusion.

And in the meantime, it is Yigal Amir's legacy, not Rabin's,
that has prevailed in Israel. In the special elections held seven
months after the murder, Benjamin Netanyahu, one of Oslo's
most violent opponents, was elected as prime minister. Before
the assassination, Netanyahu had condemned Rabin as a "traitor,"
and was photographed at a hard-right demonstration standing
next to a black coffin with RABIN KILLS ZIONISM written on
it in big letters. He was, by all means, complicit in the insidious
incitement that led to the murder. Shimon Peres, Rabin's foreign
minister running against Netanyahu on the Oslo ticket, lost mis-
erably. Netanyahu did not immediately or single-handedly

dismantle the peace process. That was a joint project, orchestrated by the powerful Israeli and Palestinian opponents of compromise—most significantly Israel's right, backed by the fundamentalist religious Zionist movement, which found natural allies in Muslim fundamentalist groups such as Hamas and the Islamic Jihad on the Palestinian side. (Moderate leaders who supported the two-state solution, such as Ehud Barak and Yasser Arafat, made some serious errors, too.) The two-state solution had been in deep trouble for a long time, but the question remained: What other hope was there? Now that Trump had freed the right of any need to pretend, the Israeli left could not afford the illusions of its own politics. Neither can the Biden administration, which faces the choice of clinging to Trump's "Deal of the Century" or promoting a genuine program for a democratic future in the country. It will not be possible to backpedal.

"Occupation" is, by international law, an irregular or transitory state of affairs. 2017 marked the fiftieth year of Israel's military regime over millions of Palestinians. In 1993, when the Oslo Agreement was first signed, approximately 260,000 settlers were living beyond the Green Line. Now, this number has grown to about 700,000 settlers.[7] Israel has filled the West Bank with settlements, highways, and infrastructure, as well as with banks, factories, businesses, and a university. In truth, we should talk of apartheid instead of occupation, for the territory has already de facto been annexed. Apologists for Israel denounce the use of the word "apartheid" as an effort to "delegitimize" the country's existence, but the country's true friends should insist on it, too. Our country needs the truth, not lies: as long as there is a taboo on describing things as they are, it will remain impossible to imagine another way.

How far advanced, how official, the annexation now is, and how unapologetically unequal it is, cannot be understated. According to Israel's Central Bureau of Statistics, the country's current population of 8.84 million people is 74.5 percent Jewish and 20.9 percent Arab. These figures include 700,000 Jews who live in the West Bank, and maps officially issued by Israel's government present that territory as integral to the country: there is no trace of the '67 border on them. The same is true of the maps in the textbooks of Israel's Ministry of Education.[8]

Not included in the population count, however, are the 3 million Palestinians who live in the West Bank. Not included on the maps are any of the Palestinian towns, cities, or villages that are to be found there.[9] In other words, the "facts" provided by Israel's Bureau of Statistics have nothing to do with the facts; they are a denial of the facts in the interest of ideology. Within the borders the Central Bureau of Statistics deems internal to Israel live approximately 11.84 million people, not 8.84 million. About 53 percent of them are Jewish, and 47 percent of them are Arab.

(With Gaza's nearly 2 million inhabitants, the majority of the population between the Jordan River and the Mediterranean is Palestinian.)

All the area on the Bureau's maps is deemed Israel, and Israeli voting law also recognizes it as such. Israeli law, unlike American law, forbids absentee voting. In order to vote, citizens must be registered at an address within Israel and must physically vote at the polling station assigned to that address. For Jewish settlers, that address *is* their West Bank address, and the West Bank is where they vote. Settlers vote there for the Israeli parliament, and they are also subject to the laws it legislates, as enforced by Israel police and judged in Israeli courts. Israeli ministers and numerous lawmakers live in the West Bank, as do Supreme Court justices. These Jewish inhabitants of the West Bank obviously live and consider themselves to live in Israel. Palestinian residents (the ones who aren't counted and aren't on the maps) live, by contrast, in an Israeli police state, under the aggressive military jurisdiction of the IDF.

The annexation is already a fact of life and the idea of its assuming permanent form as a single Jewish state is gaining ground in Israel and abroad. It is dangerous to see this idea as confined to the Zionist hard right. Israel's president, Reuven "Ruvi" Rivlin, a friendly man and a longtime political enemy of Netanyahu who has managed to establish himself as the last bastion of Israeli democratic rule of law and liberal civility, has supported it throughout his political career. Rivlin was a ferocious opponent of Oslo in Rabin's days, and he has remained an explicit and eloquent opponent of any territorial compromise or the establishment of a Palestinian state. An old-school Revisionist Zionist, Rivlin rejected Netanyahu's 2009 Bar-Ilan University speech, in which the prime minister pretended to embrace the idea that the Israelis and Palestinians should "live side by side … each with its anthem, flag, and government,"[10] and he continues to support the official annexation of the West Bank by the Jewish state. He has been called "Israel's conscience" by *The Guardian*.[11] But he has never bothered to explain how annexation can be squared with liberal democracy.

And the illusion that it *can* be—the Ruvi Rivlin Illusion, I call it—is the one that Zionists left and right are settling comfortably into. The settlement project is by now too extensive and prosperous to undo, and yet somehow a Jewish state that has annexed the West Bank and now has a 50 percent Palestinian population will remain a liberal Jewish democracy. Netanyahu must go, the minuscule remnants of Israel's left-wing parties affirm, and to achieve that, they would have no problem supporting a government formed by Naftali Bennet, the settlers' leader, with Gideon Sa'ar, a Rivlin protégé who stands even farther to the right than Netanyahu, and Avigdor Lieberman. Merav Michaeli, a self-proclaimed progressive who speaks Hebrew using predominantly feminine declensions and who, for a moment, revived the Labor Party, has declared herself unwilling to use the term "occupation," dismissing it as politically correct. Those who might call the politics of such a coalition racist—a politics of apartheid—can always be delegitimized as anti-Semites. Will the Israeli left, as well as the American Democratic Party and organizations like J Street or the New Israel Fund, go on deceiving themselves in this way, or will they offer an alternative that is true to their professed liberal democratic ideals?

2.

For those who seek a worthwhile future for both Israelis and Palestinians, one question has become unavoidable. How can Jews and Arabs live in peace in a common nation in which both peoples exercise the self-determination that both reasonably demand? Might there even be a model of such arrangement, beyond the Oslo Illusion?

The question isn't being asked. Instead time is wasted on speculation: What if Ehud Olmert, or Ehud Barak, had gone a little further? What if Rabin had lived? These vain speculations reveal nothing so much as the political taboos that today limit our political imagination. In a search for a viable model for the political future, we need to look beyond Oslo to the deeper past. As we have seen, Israel's founding fathers imagined a binational one-state solution with the Palestinians; few people know, however, that none other than Menachem Begin developed a detailed proposal for reshaping Israel in the form of a quasi-federative constellation.

Israel's first right-wing prime minister, a disciple of Jabotinsky, vehemently rejected all territorial compromise with the Palestinians. (In 1947, Ben-Gurion famously celebrated the UN's partition resolution, and Begin rejected it.) In 1977, however, when pressed by US president Jimmy Carter and Egypt's president Anwar Sadat to offer a peace plan to the Palestinians as part of a comprehensive peace agreement with Egypt, Begin proposed a surprising program. Titled "Home Rule, for Palestinian Arabs, Residents of Judea, Samaria and the Gaza District," it granted the Palestinians self-determination—but without dividing the country. Presented to the Americans and Egyptians on December 15, 1977, the plan was initially kept as top secret. It was also "Subject to the Confirmation of the Government of Israel."[12]

Begin's plan provided for the "abolition" of military rule in the West Bank and Gaza; it was to be replaced by an autonomous Palestinian authority "of the residents, by and for them." The authority would be overseen by a council, elected every four years by standard democratic procedures and exercising jurisdiction over all aspects of civil life through Departments of Education, Health, Finance, Transportation, Housing, Religion, Police, Welfare, Tourism, Agriculture, and Commerce. Especially significant was the inclusion on the list of a Department of Rehabilitation of Refugees.

The plan did not offer the Palestinians a sovereign state, but it did something unimaginable today—and this why we must heed it: it offered full citizenship to every Palestinian, every one of whom would be "entitled to vote for, and be elected to, the Knesset." To Israelis it guaranteed full freedom of movement and economic liberties in the West Bank and Gaza, conceding likewise that Palestinians would be free to live, settle, work, and purchase land on the full territory. Often called the "Autonomy Program," Begin's plan could just as well have been known as the "One-State Program."

Today most Israelis are unaware that this plan ever existed, much less that it offered Palestinians not only autonomy, but citizenship. This fact is not so much overlooked as put out of mind. Such a thing, it is presumed, simply could not have been. Israelis grasp correctly that to offer autonomy is to offer something less than a state—so far, the story makes sense—but to offer it with full Israeli citizenship would be to approach the sort of binational federation that Amos Oz, as we have seen, derided as an absurdity. And so, allegedly, Begin could not have possibly offered *that*.

He did, however, and it should be acknowledged that some historians who were aware that he did have sought to downplay the significance of the deed. Nathan Thrall, one of the most important commentators on Israeli politics in English, defended the viability of the two-state solution in his 2016 *The Only Language They Understand* while characterizing Begin's program as an "interesting" anecdote.[13] Seth Anziska, who has conducted the latest and most important historical research on the program, nonetheless treats it primarily as a plot to "prevent Palestine," designed to undermine the Palestinians' aspiration to national sovereignty.[14] "The recent revival of interest in the autonomy plan among right-wing politicians in Israel," Anziska writes, "attests to the deep imprint it continues to have on Israel's approach to the Palestinians."[15] But whereas Israeli right-wing politicians may be interested in autonomy plans, it is safe to say that none of them wishes to revive the features that make this one so unique. The idea of granting Palestinians citizenship is as entirely unacceptable to right-wing politicians as it is inconceivable to the most liberal of liberal Zionists, who prefer to cling to Oslo, whatever the cost, in order to avoid doing just that. Begin was undoubtedly intent on "preventing Palestine," but that does not change the fact that an arrangement similar—but by no means identical—to the one he proposed has by now become the only way for Jews and Palestinians to live together and enjoy full national and individual equality between the Jordan River and the Mediterranean.

Critics on the left might object that granting Palestinians Israeli citizenship is unsatisfactory because, in a Jewish state, sovereignty in any case lies with the Jewish people rather than with citizens as such. But this is to fail to perceive the revolutionary potential of the program: by offering citizenship to Palestinians, Begin's plan doesn't just downgrade Palestinian sovereignty into self-determination; no, it also transforms the nature of sovereignty in Israel—expanding it beyond the idea of exclusive Jewish sovereignty. A state in which all Palestinians are offered full citizenship is one that has taken the main step towards becoming a republic that belongs to all its citizens.

After presenting the plan in secret to Sadat and Carter, Begin submitted it to the Knesset for approval on December 28, 1977. In a dramatic speech, the prime minister himself read it out line by line and defended it from the podium. There were a few significant deviations from the original document, some concessions to American and Egyptian demands. A clause had been added addressing the right of return:

A committee will be established of representatives of Israel, Jordan, and the [Palestinian] Administrative Council to determine norms of immigration to the areas of Judea, Samaria and the Gaza district. The committee will determine the norms whereby Arab refugees residing outside Judea, Samaria and the Gaza district will be permitted to immigrate to these areas in reasonable numbers. The rulings of the committee will be adopted by unanimous decision.[16]

This statement both enhanced and limited the powers of the autonomous authority's Department of Rehabilitation of Refugees. It enhanced it because it stated clearly that rehabilitation would include physical return. And it limited it by specifying that this would happen in "reasonable" numbers that would not depend on the department's jurisdiction alone. Note, however, that Arabs constitute the majority of an Israeli-Palestinian-Jordanian committee; note, too, that Palestinians voting as Israeli citizens were in a position to shape the Israeli portion of the committee. Above all, returning refugees would be offered full citizenship and the freedom to move, purchase land, and settle on the whole territory. The clause supplied an explicit platform from which to begin to address the Palestinians' right of return to the territories that they had been expelled from during the Nakba.

Another new clause addressed the question of sovereignty in the West Bank and Gaza:

> Israel stands by its right and its claim of sovereignty to Judea, Samaria and the Gaza district. In the knowledge that other claims exist, it proposes, for the sake of the agreement and peace, that the question of sovereignty in these areas be left open.[17]

Anziska writes that in his Knesset speech Begin "implored, 'We have a right and a demand for sovereignty over these areas of *Eretz Yisrael....* This is our land and it belongs to the Jewish nation rightfully.'"[18] But while emphasizing Israel's *claim* to sovereignty, the clause Begin brought for the Knesset's approval actually recognized the existence of competing claims, and left the question of sovereignty open—as Begin explained before the vote. This assertion of sovereignty was also an admission of the legitimacy of other claims of sovereignty. This was equivocal, of course, but—and this is the most important thing—in addressing the Knesset Begin was entirely unequivocal about the offer of full citizenship to Palestinians. He said:

> And now I want to explain why we proposed a free choice of citizenship, including Israeli citizenship ... again the answer is: Fairness ... we never wanted to be like Rhodesia. And this is a

way to show our fairness to all men of goodwill ... here we propose total equality of rights—anti-racialism—of course, if they chose such citizenship ... we do not force our citizenship on anyone.[19]

Rhodesia—after 1979, Zimbabwe—was a white-supremacist state in 1977. Effectively, Israel's prime minister was warning from the podium of the Knesset that if Israel did not grant Palestinian citizenship, it would be guilty of Jewish apartheid. And this indeed was the note on which Begin concluded his speech: "Mr. Speaker, the debate has ended. I ask for a vote, and I ask that each and every member of the Knesset, without distinction of faction, vote according to his conscience. There is no imposition, no coercion. I am confident of the result."[20] On the questions of giving autonomous authority to the Palestinians in Gaza and the West Bank; of leaving the issue of full sovereignty in these territories open; of offering to every Palestinian the option of full Israeli citizenship; of recognizing the right of return of Palestinian refugees "in reasonable numbers"; and of granting the right to full economic liberty and freedom of movement throughout the whole territory to both Jews and Palestinians, Israel's Knesset voted sixty-four in favor and eight against. Forty abstained. The program was approved.

If one looks at this result with the Oslo Agreement in mind, it seems utterly anomalous. And yet it is, as I have shown, continuous with the fundamental tenets of Zionist thinking up to the mid-1930s: before the Holocaust made Zionist politics a zero-sum game that required an ethnic notion of citizenship; before transfer and separation, required for homogeneous national sovereignty, became the dominant agenda.

3.

But of course, Begin's plan came to nothing. The Palestinians, seeking sovereignty, rejected it, and the Israelis were glad to back-pedal once it became clear that they could have peace with Egypt without giving the Palestinians anything. Accordingly, much of the commentary on Begin's plan considers it a step on the way to Oslo's failed Palestinian Authority. Here, however, I would like to suggest we look at it as a step *beyond* Oslo.

One might propose a one-state solution along the following lines, reconstructed from Begin's program:

1. The military occupation of the West Bank and the military isolation of the Gaza Strip will be terminated. Two states, Israel and Palestine, will exist as a single federation on the territory between the Jordan River and the Mediterranean Sea, their separate jurisdiction marked by the 1967 Green Line. Within

each state, each of the peoples, the Jews and the Palestinians, will exercise cultural and national self-determination.

2. The unity of the two states will be determined and ensured by a joint constitution, to which each state's legislative, executive, and judicial branches will be subject. The constitution will guarantee universal human rights and basic liberties: the separation of church and state; democratic elections; neutral rule of law and individual equality regardless of race, religion, gender, or citizenship; and full recognition of the Jews' and the Palestinians' national rights.

3. The constitution will also ensure the existence of the following rights and institutions:

   a) Freedom of movement. The borders between the two states will be open. Full freedom of movement will be guaranteed on the whole territory. Israel's citizens will be able to travel freely in Palestine's territories; Palestine's citizens will be able to travel freely in Israel's territory.

   b) Economic freedom. Citizens of Israel will have the right to live, work, and buy land on the whole territory. Citizens of Palestine will have the right to live, work, and buy land on the whole territory.

4. Each state will be responsible for its own internal security. Their security forces will be joined by a mutual defense treaty. A common steering council will regulate the common security

interests of both states, as well as the defense of their common external borders.

5. Israel's citizens, regardless of their place of residence, will vote for the Knesset. Palestine's citizens, regardless of their place of residence, will vote for Palestine's parliament. Their basic national rights, for example education, will be ensured by the constitution in their place of residence.

6. Arabic and Hebrew will be official languages in both states. Arabic will be taught as an obligatory second language in Israeli schools. Hebrew will be taught as an obligatory second language in Palestinian schools.

7. Both the Holocaust and the Nakba will be commemorated in public, jointly by Jews and Palestinians, under the auspice of joint research institutions. Israeli schoolchildren will study the Nakba and commemorate it together with Palestinian students. Palestinian schoolchildren will study the Holocaust and commemorate it together with Jewish students.

8. The right of return of both Jews and Palestinians will be recognized by both states. Jews will be able to naturalize as Israel's citizens; Palestinians as Palestine's citizens. Since each state's citizens will enjoy full liberties on the whole territory, a joint steering committee will establish the norms for immigration of Jews to Israel and Palestinians to Palestine.

9. The capital of Israel will be in West Jerusalem. The capital of Palestine will be in East Jerusalem.

10. A joint constitutional Supreme Court of Appeals will be established, overseeing the operation of each state's legislative, executive, and judicial branches, as well as of the joint committees of security and immigration.

11. There will be equal representation of Jews and Palestinians in the joint Supreme Court, and in the steering committees. These will be located in Haifa.

Obviously, such a scheme presents complications. Specific questions of security, economy, water, and borders, among many others, will have to be negotiated, planned concretely, deliberated publicly, and approved with the support of world powers. The same, however, is true of the two-state vision: before it gained its current status, it was almost universally considered a heresy, an impossible anti-Zionist fantasy and a half-baked suggestion by dreamy intellectuals. The same will by definition be true of any forward-looking alternative to the Oslo paradigm, now that it really has become impossible. The merit of this alternative is that it opens a path to securing human rights and the rights of citizenship on the whole territory, without denying the historical aspirations of both Jews and Palestinians to exercise self-determination and national rights. Thus it also reflects a conviction that Zionism, the aspiration to Jewish self-determination, can have a viable and honorable political future in the twenty-first century, if, that is, it can be reinvented along familiar but forgotten lines from its past. Because if it is not, Israel will become a twenty-first-century Rhodesia, with Jewish supremacism legally and publicly established as a norm.

4.

But is there a political future for the sort of binational vision I have described? Readers may well be skeptical, but in this regard we should take into account Rabin's example. After Oslo, Netanyahu accused him of wanting to "kill Zionism," which is ridiculous when you consider *what* Rabin was attempting, which was to preserve Jewish demographic superiority by territorial compromise. However, when you look at the unprecedented *way* in which Rabin pushed Oslo through the Knesset, the reason for Netanyahu's alarm becomes apparent, as do the grounds for hope in a democratic future for Israel.

Palestinian Israelis are of course allowed to stand as candidates in Israel's elections, but they have never been accepted as equal political subjects. The clearest expression of their exclusion is that they have never been invited to join government coalitions. In fact, all mainstream Israeli parties explicitly assure their voters that they would not join coalitions that do not enjoy a "Jewish majority." The significance of this norm cannot be overstated; it is so ironclad an understanding that it may as well have been written into the constitution, and it ensures that sovereignty in Israel is kept in Jewish hands.

There has, however, been one exception to this rule in the history of Israel. Rabin lacked a Jewish majority for Oslo, but he refused to back off. Instead, he relied on the Arab parties, who agreed to support his coalition from the outside in order to push the two-state solution through the Knesset. For the first and last time in Israeli history, a bill—and not *just* any bill, but the decision to end the occupation and establish a Palestinian state—was passed not by Jewish sovereignty but by the sovereignty of its citizens as a whole.

Accepting the full equal political status of Arab Israelis: this is Rabin's true Oslo legacy, genuinely democratic and revolutionary in potential, and one that we must heed now that the two-state solution lies buried. Liberal Zionists who support Oslo often repeat the idea that "the unity of the people is more important than the unity of the land," implying that it is better to divide the Holy Land than to divide the Jewish people. Rabin's actions in Oslo directly contravened this pious slogan: in this case he was willing to sacrifice the unity of the land *and that* of the Jewish people. The iconic general, who in 1948 gave orders to expel whole Palestinian cities—and later suggested "breaking the arms and legs" of Palestinians throwing stones in the Intifada—took a radical turn. Arguably, it was this "betrayal" of Jewish sovereignty, as much as territorial compromise in the Holy Land, that led to Rabin being portrayed as a traitor and a Nazi collaborator, and to his eventual murder.

Yes, Rabin no doubt supposed this one sacrifice and the division of the territory would secure Jewish sovereignty in the future. His intentions, however, do not matter. We must see past them to the logic of citizenship that was driving his actions. And by the end of his life, Rabin had come to understand that there was nothing treasonous about realist democratic politics. He grasped that defending Israeli democracy on the strength of Jewish majority alone is impossible: first, because the numbers just don't add up; second, because defending democracy by a Jewish majority alone is a contradiction in terms. A liberal democratic agenda must concede the full equality of Arab citizens.

This legacy of Rabin's is the necessary foundation for Israel's democratic future. Parliamentary Jewish-Palestinian collaboration offers a prospect of adapting and improving on the Begin plan, replacing the two-state solution with a binational federation. The purpose of a joint Palestinian-Jewish politics must be cohabitation, not separation, and the prospect of a transformation that can reinvigorate Israeli politics anew. Indeed, when we consider the logic that motivated Israel's two greatest post-1967 leaders at the moments at which they broke taboos in pursuit of peace, we see that both of them touched that deeper logic, that both were returning to Zionism's initial commitment to Arab-Jewish cohabitation, and that, as Ben-Gurion himself stated a hundred years ago, when a binational program was still his program: "All other notions undermine our existence in Palestine."[21] We must reconnect to this legacy, on the Jewish and the Palestinian side, and begin offering it as a hope for the future.

For two decades now, the political hopes of the Israeli left have dwindled with the dwindling prospect of a two-state solution. The right has established a hegemony and the liberal Zionist opposition, with no realistic alternative of its own, has lost all credibility. This opposition is by now a ghost from the past, associated with figures like Amos Oz and David Grossman rather than domestic politicians of real stature. Progressive American Jews, and perhaps a few EU officials, like to believe in it. It has virtually no standing in Israel's parliament.

Yet the political ruin in which Israel's left now lies can be seen, paradoxically, as a reason for optimism. Once we have disposed of the Oslo Illusion it will become increasingly clear that a liberal Zionist political alternative can only emerge through an organic joint politics of Palestinian Israelis and Jews. In March 2020, the previous round of Israeli elections, a growing number of liberal Jews voted for the increasingly influential Arab Joint List instead of wasting their votes on the moribund Labor or Meretz Parties—people like my father, a lifelong leftist Zionist, a reserve officer in the Israel Defense Forces, and the son of Holocaust survivors. Meretz, the last bastion of Zionist two-state supporters, saw many of its voters turn to the Joint List, and this was a crossing of the Rubicon: having identified as Zionists their whole lives, these voters had certainly never imagined casting a vote for a non-Zionist Arab party.

Precisely how many Jews crossed over is hard to say since many of them live in mixed urban centers such as Haifa, Jerusalem, and Tel Aviv. We do know, however, that in the election of September 2020, the Joint List received 9,918 votes in areas where Jews constitute at least 75 percent of the population. Five months later, in the same areas, it more than doubled its take, to 20,652 votes. In absolute numbers, this doesn't sound like much, but it is much more significant than it seems. Israel is small to begin with, and left-liberal voters comprise a small fraction of it. (*Haaretz*, for example, has about 65,000 subscribers.)

In any case, a growing turnout of Arab voters and a surge of first-time Jewish supporters made this the Joint List's best result in Israel's history. With fifteen seats, it became the sole party on the left standing in opposition to the Netanyahu-led government. At a subsequent anti-annexation rally in Rabin Square in Tel Aviv—the place where the prime minister was assassinated after a massive Oslo peace rally—the list's leader, Ayman Odeh, was easily the most significant Israeli politician to speak: he emerged as the leader of Israel's anti-occupation camp. Delivering the main speech, he declared:

> We are at a crossroads. One path leads to a joint society with a real democracy, civil and national equality for Arab citizens.... The second path leads to hatred, violence, annexation and apartheid.... We're here, in Rabin Square, to pick the first path.[22]

The US Senator Bernie Sanders followed Odeh with a recorded video message. "In the words of my friend Ayman Odeh," he said, "the only future is a shared future."[23] Sanders may not be the US president, but his words are sure to represent the thinking of many younger American Democrats, and there will be growing pressure to make this the party's agenda. The sooner it does, the better.

In advance of the March 2020 elections, opinion pieces in *Haaretz* showed more and more Jewish support for the Joint

List, leading the paper's editor-in-chief, Aluf Benn, to respond with a column dismissing the trend toward "civil equality between the Jordan River and the Sea" in the words of Dmitry Shumsky, one of *Haaretz*'s top political commentators, as "messianic"—a leftist delusion.[24] Shumsky in turn dismissed Benn's argument as based on a "false political picture." The Joint List, he averred, supports the idea of separate states. A vote for the list, he argued, is a vote for the two-state solution—an idea that remains the only "rational" choice, as "utopian" as it now seems.[25]

That is true for now, but if the emerging collaboration of Arabs and Jews is to succeed in filling the vacuum left by the disappearance of liberal Zionist parties, it will have to go beyond that position. As we've seen, clinging to the two-state solution is not so much rational as a willful denial of the facts, while the sort of purely tactical politics that Shumsky has advocated here will hardly suffice to build full civil equality in one state. That work will be difficult, but it is not at all "messianic" to do it; we must engage in it for real and without reserve. We can look to the past, as I have shown, for an example—to the original Zionists, to the Begin plan—but above all we must build trust in the present for the future. That is what the Joint List has it in it to do and must set out to do. When Jewish Israelis vote for the list, they are not just expressing but constructing trust. They demonstrate that we can already imagine a bridge to a binational project independent of ethnic identity, one that will take us beyond the alleged necessity of separation.

Over recent years, the Joint List has invested much energy in cultivating this trust. One need only consider the name, designed to dispel the notion that it is an exclusively Arab bloc: while Israel's constantly re-forming center-left parties have in recent years gone for patriotic, not to say nationalist, names—the Zionist Union, Blue and White, the Israel Resilience Party—this historically Arab grouping branded itself in Hebrew as *Ha'meshutefet*, meaning "the shared" or "the common." And during a recent Democracy Conference convened by *Haaretz*, the list's leader, Ayman Odeh, pointed out that the bloc's chief "handicap" is that it has too many Arab representatives: it needs more prominent Jews.[26] And speeches like the one Ahmad Tibi, a leading figure of the list, delivered on Holocaust Memorial Day should be a regular event: to Jewish voters like my father they signal that Arab members of the Knesset can and already do recognize and represent them and their history. Indeed, at the most recent Holocaust Memorial Ceremony conducted at the Knesset, Tibi made a point of leaving the hall during Itamar Ben-Gvir's speech: he would not tolerate an open fascist commemorating the Holocaust, and he was making it clear once again that memory is too important to be abused. The Jewish representatives of such a list, and indeed any other list on the left, must commemorate the

Holocaust with the same integrity—and by the same token of integrity must promote laws for the full civil commemoration of the Nakba.

For the time being, the Joint List remains isolated in Israel. It took a hit in the last round of elections, as the Arab voting percentage went down drastically. And, in the coalition discussions following all the recent general elections, the parties of the center-left preferred to ally themselves with the prime minister's party or with hard-right politicians like Sa'ar, Lieberman, and Bennett rather than to join forces with Arab lawmakers. Yet the inescapable if remarkable conclusion is that the Joint List is the best—really, the only—representation in Israeli politics, not only for bereft liberal Zionist voters but also for progressive pro-Israel international Jewish organizations such as J Street and the New Israel Fund, and the same is true for the Democratic Party and for the European Union. The international community would do well to start recognizing that a joint Arab-Jewish politics is *the only model* for a democratic future in Israel—and the only model that propels the country beyond the two-state solution. It is time to start lending this nascent politics legitimacy and support.

With strong turnout, Arab voters alone can account for almost twenty parliament seats, and with a slate that includes a new generation of charismatic Jewish candidates who can campaign effectively in Hebrew and gain the support of liberal Zionist voters, the list could arguably win up to five more seats. This will not be enough to form a governing coalition, but it could well be enough to make the Joint List the largest opposition party in the Knesset and the country's designated opposition leader.

Israeli law gives this role significant powers. According to the Knesset Law, 1994, the prime minister must consult the opposition leader on vital state matters "as necessary, and no less than once a month." The opposition leader also has the right to speak immediately after the prime minister in the Knesset and at all official ceremonies. For the leader of an Arab-Jewish coalition to play this part, and enjoy international backing, is a development that would carry enormous weight and help bring into being an alternative binational vision.

Let us call this binational vision the Haifa Republic. For too long, the competing models of Jerusalem and Tel Aviv have over-shadowed Haifa as a symbol of what Israel can and should be. Jerusalem is the symbol of Jewish longing, a sacred city for Muslims, Christians, and Jews, but it is also an idol, in the worst sense of the term, worshipped by nationalist and religious fundamentalists. Tel Aviv, capital of the Hebrew state, is a vibrant, liberal, secular Jewish beach town, but is just as much as Jerusalem a golden calf, a false promise—in this case of what liberal Jewish life could look like if Jews could live only among themselves. As if a liberal city worthy of the name wouldn't necessarily be post-ethnic.

Haifa represents a different model, and despite appearances, a more ambitious one: for it is in Haifa, not Jerusalem or Tel Aviv, that you get a glimpse of what Palestinian-Jewish cohabitation could one day look like. In Haifa, a true experiment in civil living is going on. In Haifa's hospitals, among them some of the best in the country, Arab and Jewish doctors work together treating the north's heavily mixed population. Here Arab and Jewish patients lie side by side. At Haifa University, more than any other university in Israel, a program of binational, bilingual research, and higher education is actually conceivable, and an Arabic-language Israeli theater, Al-Midan, already operates in the city. The Israeli novelist most associated with Haifa is Sami Michael, an Iraqi Jew who speaks Arabic as his mother tongue and whose work, unlike Oz's, boldly tests and extends Israeli identity: Michael's *Pigeons in Trafalgar* tells the story of an Israeli adopted child who discovers his Palestinian mother—and how as a Palestinian raised by Jews he is heir to both the trauma of the Holocaust and the trauma of the Nakba. In this novel, Michael is responding to an an earlier short story, "Returning to Haifa," by Ghassan Kanafani, which describes a Palestinian couple who escape Haifa and the Nakba to the West Bank: in doing so, they leave their infant child behind and only in 1967 are they able to return and look for him. (Kanafani, a member of the Popular Front for the Liberation of Palestine, was assassinated by the Mossad in 1972.)

In the Arab-owned cafes of Haifa's Masada Street, in the city's Jewish Quarter, the true cosmopolitan potential of the place emerges most dramatically: here Arab and Jewish neighbors converge as a matter of course; here their lives cross, friendships are formed, people fall in love. Similarly, Maccabi Haifa, the city's soccer team and one of the strongest in the country, features Arab and Jewish players side by side in its Hall of Fame, and not just the players but even its fans are both Palestinian Israelis and Jewish. Since soccer is never just soccer, compare Maccabi Haifa to Beitar Jerusalem, Jerusalem's team infamous for refusing to accept Arab players, its fans chanting that Beitar will remain "pure forever."

People sometimes speak with nostalgia of the long-gone world of Jerusalem's Old City, where in the days of the empires, before Israel was established, a spirit of neighborliness reigned. In some parts of Haifa this is not a question of nostalgia; that spirit is present and active and a utopian inspiration. Cynics might retort that the struggles of day-to-day life in this hardly high-flying city are anything but utopian. Others may dislike the claim that the city presents a model of equal Jewish and Arab cohabitation, so let us be clear: it doesn't. Still, the glimpses it gives of a common life are all the more astonishing in light of the Israeli-Palestinian conflict that surrounds them. If Israel is to have a civilized—and not just civilized but exciting—future, it will grow out of the kind of civic life lived in Haifa.

And Haifa is meaningful for another reason. Here we see not only a possible future but the possibility of both remembering and forgetting the past. The city's port is one of the most important gates through which the *ma'apilim*—Jewish refugees who escaped Europe on overcrowded boats and had to be smuggled past the British authorities—came to Palestine. At the same time, Haifa was the site of one of the most traumatic moments of the Nakba—in which the city's inhabitants fled by boat en masse, a critical moment in the collapse of Palestinian society. Emile Habibi, whose "Your Holocaust, Our Nakba" I quoted in chapter 3, asked that his grave be inscribed: REMAINED IN HAIFA.

Yes, the Haifa Republic seems like a dream now, but it is an old-new dream that Jews and Palestinians must learn to dream together. Despite appearances, the elements to make it a reality exist: in our history, in the Knesset, in life as it is lived in Haifa even today. We can and must work with them, for if we do not, reality will become a nightmare. If you will it, said Herzl, it is not a dream. It is time to will that this dream, like the land, will belong to both peoples together.

Notes

INTRODUCTION

1. Numbers are based on Peace Now's "Settlement Watch," https://peacenow.org.il/settlements-watch/matzav/population, and on Shaul Arieli's *Messianism Meets Reality: The Israeli Settlement Project in Judea and Samaria: Vision or Illusion, 1967–2016* (Tel Aviv: Economic Cooperation Foundation, 2017), which draws on the official figures provided by the Israel Bureau of Statistics.

2. The quote is Nathan Thrall's, in his *The Only Language They Understand: Forcing Compromise in Israel and Palestine* (New York: Metropolitan Books, 2017), 70. Arieli supports the same thesis in *Messianism Meets Reality*. For a recent, and more elaborate, statement of this argument, see Susie Linfield, *The Lions' Den: Zionism and the Left from Hannah Arendt and Noam Chomsky* (New Haven: Yale University Press, 2019).

3. "Meeting between Ministerial Committee for Autonomy Talks and U.S. Special Ambassador, Mr. Sol Linowitz, September 2, 1980,

Cabinet Room, Prime Minister's Office, Jerusalem" [in Hebrew], A-4316/14, Israel State Archives, Jerusalem [ISA]. Unless otherwise noted, all translations from foreign-language texts are my own.

4. Benjamin Netanyahu, "Address by PM Netanyahu at Bar-Ilan University," Israel Ministry of Foreign Affairs (website), June 14, 2009.

5. Eyal Levi, "Interview with Amiram Levin: Next Time We Fight, The Palestinians Will Not Stay Here, We Will Kick Them To the Other Side of the Jordan" [in Hebrew], *Maariv*, December 13, 2017.

6. Amichai Atali, "Smotrich: Concur Gaza Anew, and Open its Gates to a Massive Emigration" [in Hebrew], *Ynet* (*Yedioth Ahronoth*), March 29, 2019.

7. Amos Oz, *Dear Zealots: Letters from a Divided Land*, trans. Jessica Cohen (New York: Houghton Mifflin Harcourt, 2018), 127.

8. Oz, 130–32.

9. Antonio Gramsci, *Selections from the Prison Notebooks*, eds. Quentin Hoare and Geoffrey Nowell-Smith (London: Lawrence and Wishart, 1971), 276.

10. Tony Judt, "Israel: The Alternative," *The New York Review of Books*, December 4, 2003.

11. Leon Wieseltier, "Israel, Palestine and the Return of the Bi-National Fantasy: What Is Not to be Done," *The New Republic*, October 27, 2003.

12. Michael Walzer, letter to the editor, *The New York Review of Books*, December 4, 2003.

13. Thomas Friedman, "The Many Mideast Solutions," *The New York Times*, February 10, 2016.

14. Friedman, "President Trump, Will You Save the Jews?," *The New York Times*, February 15, 2017.

15. Peter Beinart, "I No Longer Believe in a Jewish State," *The New York Times*, July 8, 2020; Alan Dershowitz, "Beinart's Final Solution: End Israel as Nation-State of the Jewish People," *Newsweek*, July 14, 2020.

16. Michelle Goldberg, "Is Liberal Zionism Dead?," *The New York Times*, January 9, 2018.

17. This thesis has received in recent years increasing attention, but was powerfully and comprehensively elaborated by Dmitry Shumsky in *Beyond the Nation-State: The Zionist Political Imagination from Pinsker to Ben-Gurion* (New Haven: Yale University Press, 2018). Michael Brenner has made a similar case in *In Search of Israel: The History of an Idea* (Princeton: Princeton University Press, 2018).

18. Vladimir Jabotinsky, "On Binational Palestine" [in Russian], *Rassvet*, January 3, 1926. Translation from Dmitry Shumsky, *Beyond the Nation-State*, 90–91.

19. For full quotes and references, see chapter 3.

20. For a truly groundbreaking collection of essays, jointly discussing the Holocaust and the Nakba, see Bashir Bashir and Amos Goldberg, eds., *The Holocaust and the Nakba: A New Grammar of Trauma and History* (New York: Columbia University Press, 2018). The editors are correct, in my view, that seeking a language to discuss the links between these two foundational histories, without blurring the differences between them, is necessary for binational political visions. As Alon Confino wrote in his review of the book's earlier Hebrew edition, its main significance lies in the performative act of its writing: "This is the real event and the significant effort. This act in itself generates a jolt, without which there is no prospect of national rights and human rights for all the inhabitants of the land" (H-Soz-u-Kult, H-Net Reviews, April 2016).

21. Ernest Renan, "What is a Nation?," in *What is a Nation? and Other Political Writings*, trans. and ed. M. F. N. Giglioli (New York: Columbia University Press, 2018), 247–63.

22. See Avraham Burg's memoir, *In Days to Come, A New Hope for Israel* (New York: Nation Books, 2018), and most significantly, the website for Meron Rapoport and Awni Al-Mashni's joint Israeli-Palestinian initiative, Two States, One Homeland.

CHAPTER 1
THE LIBERAL ZIONISM OF THE FUTURE

1. Ornan v. Ministry of the Interior, CA 8573/08, October 2, 2013.

2. Moshe Halbertal, "Is a Jewish and Democratic State Possible?" [in Hebrew], *Haaretz*, April 27, 2013. Unless otherwise noted, all quotes from Halbertal are from this article. The essay is de facto a reply to Eva Illouz's earlier *Haaretz* intervention, "Is Israel Too Jewish?" [in English], March 23, 2013, which had criticized his position. Illouz's essay was reprinted in German in *Israel* (Berlin: Suhrkamp Verlag, 2015), 46–62.

3. Avishai Margalit and Moshe Halbertal, "Liberalism and the Right to Culture," *Social Research* 61, no. 3 (1994): 491.

4. Margalit and Halbertal, 492.

5. Andrew Pessin has argued this in a *Times of Israel* op-ed: "'Liberal Zionism' in the New York Times," December 28, 2016. (Full disclosure: this op-ed was written as a critique, not to say a personal attack, against my *New York Times* op-ed, "Liberal Zionism in the Age of Trump," December 20, 2016.)

6. Illouz suggests that a Jewish state that could be *represented* by an

Arab would come closer to satisfying liberal conditions. But it is at least logically possible that those who do not partake in Jewish sovereignty could represent Jewish sovereignty.

7. All quotes are drawn from the full English text printed by *Haaretz*: David Grossman, "Israel is a Fortress, but Not Yet a Home," April 18, 2018.

8. "Full Transcript: Second 2016 Presidential Debate," *Politico*, October 10, 2016.

9. Yair Rosenberg, "Richard Spencer Says He Just Wants 'White Zionism.' Here's Why That's Malicious Nonsense," *Tablet*, August 18, 2017.

10. Josh Nathan-Kazis, "'Alt Right' Leader Ties White Supremacy to Zionism—Leaves Rabbi Speechless," *Forward*, December 7, 2016.

11. Nathan-Kazis, "'Alt-Right Leader Ties White Supremacy to Zionism." See also the Twitter video of the encounter at https://twitter.com/theeagle/status/806231941167063044.

12. Ann Coulter, ¡*Adios, America!: The Left's Plan to Turn Our Country Into a Third World Hellhole* (Washington: Regnery Publishing, 2015), 18–19.

13. Pessin, "'Liberal Zionism' in The New York Times."

14. "Far-Right Austrian Leader Visits Israel's Holocaust Memorial," *Reuters*, April 12, 2016.

15. Shlomo Papierblat, "Geert Wilders Investigated by Dutch Secret Service for Ties to Israel, Report Says," *Haaretz*, December 10, 2016.

16. Aaron Klein, "Alan Dershowitz Defends Steve Bannon: 'Not Legitimate To Call Somebody An Anti-Semite Because You Disagree With Their Policies,'" *Breitbart*, November 15, 2016.

17. "Full Text: Trump's Comments on White Supremacists, 'Alt-Left' in Charlottesville," *Politico*, August 15, 2017.

18. "Echoing Trump, Israeli Ambassador Dermer Blames 'Both Sides' for Anti-Semitism," *Haaretz*, October 29, 2018.

19. Appendix 11 [in German and English] in David Yisraeli, *The Palestine Problem in German Politics, 1889–1945* (Ramat Gan: Bar Ilan University, 1974), 315–17.

20. The Declaration of the Establishment of the State of Israel, May 14, 1948. The official English translation can be found on the Israel Ministry of Foreign Affairs's website.

21. Basic Law: Israel, the Nation State of the Jewish People, enacted July 19, 2018. An unofficial English translation can found on the Israel Ministry of Foreign Affairs's website.

22. Basic Law: The Knesset, 1958. The official English translation can be found on the Israel Ministry of Foreign Affairs's website.

23. Karl Loewenstein provides the classic formulation of the doctrine, responding directly to the predicament of the Weimar Republic: "Militant Democracy and Fundamental Rights, I/II," *The American Political Science Review* 31, no. 3–4 (1937): 417–32; 638–58.

24. "MK Tibi: Israel Is Democratic for Jews and Jewish for Arabs," *The Jerusalem Post*, October 10, 2010.

25. Peter Beinart, *The Crisis of Zionism* (New York: Henry Holt, 2013), 169–70.

26. Amos Elon, for example, claims that Herzl underwent a "dramatic shift" in *The Old New Land*, setting him apart from nationalists (*Herzl* [New York: Holt, Rinehart & Winston, 1975], 348). Shlomo Avineri, by contrast, argues that Herzl was simply invoking Strauss-style esoteric writing methods (my term), averting the ire of the Ottoman censor (*Herzl: Theodor Herzl and the Foundations of the Jewish State* [London: Weidenfeld and Nicolson, 2013], 185).

NOTES TO CHAPTER 1

27. My discussion is indebted to Dmitry Shumsky's important *Beyond the Nation-State: The Zionist Political Imagination from Pinsker to Ben-Gurion* (New Haven: Yale University Press, 2018), 89.

28. Theodor Herzl, February 23, 1896, diary entry, *The Complete Diaries of Theodor Herzl*, vol. 1, ed. Raphael Patai, trans. Harry Zohn (New York: Herzl Press, 1960), 305–306.

29. Ahad Ha'am, "Introduction to New Edition," in *Ahad Ha'am: Complete Writings* [in Hebrew] (Tel Aviv: Dvir, 1947), 8–10.

30. Vladimir Jabotinsky, "On Binational Palestine" [in Russian], *Rassvet*, January 3, 1926. Translation from Dmitry Shumsky, *Beyond the Nation-State*, 90–91.

31. Jabotinsky, *The Jewish War Front* (London: Georg Allen & Unwin, 1940), 217–18.

32. David Ben-Gurion, "National Autonomy and Neighbors' Relations," in *Us and Our Neighbors* [in Hebrew] (Tel Aviv: Am Oved, 1931), 111–14. Translation from Shumsky, 196–97.

33. Ben-Gurion, "National Autonomy," 122–23. Translation slightly modified from Shumsky, 197.

34. Ben-Gurion, "Assumptions for Determining a Governmental Regime in Palestine," in *Us and Our Neighbors*, 195–96. Translation from Shumsky, 199–200.

35. Hannah Arendt, *The Jewish Writings*, eds. Jerome Kohn and Ron Feldman (New York: Schocken Books, 2007), 401.

36. See Oz's lecture at Tel Aviv University, his last public appearance, at https://www.youtube.com/watch?v=A6DXUiZhRow (in Hebrew).

37. Ben-Gurion, July 12, 1937, diary entry [in Hebrew], Ben-Gurion Archives, Ben-Gurion University of the Negev, Beersheba, Israel. Translation from Benny Morris, *The Birth of the Palestinian Refugee*

Problem Revisited (Cambridge: Cambridge University Press, 2004), 47.

38. Ben-Gurion, "Response Words in the Twenty-Second Zionist Congress" in *Ba'Ma'aracha*, vol. 5 [in Hebrew] (Tel Aviv: Am Oved, 1957), 149.

39. Ernest Renan, "What is a Nation?" in *What is a Nation? and Other Political Writings*, trans. and ed. M. F. N. Giglioli (New York: Columbia University Press, 2018), 247–63, esp. 261–62. For an account of Renan's formulation as a modern rather than romantic nationalism, see Aleida Assmann, *The Long Shadow of the Past: Cultural Memory and the Politics of History* [in German] (Munich: C. H. Beck, 2016), 39–40.

40. Renan, 251. Translation modified; the duty implied by Renan's "*doit avoir oublié*" is better understood as "ought" than "must."

41. Benedict Anderson, *Imagined Communities: Reflections on the Origin and Spread of Nationalism* (New York: Verso, 2016), 200.

42. See Ross Poole, "Enacting Oblivion," *International Journal of Politics, Culture, and Society* 22, no. 2 (2009): 149–57.

CHAPTER 2
FORGETTING AND REMEMBERING: THE HOLOCAUST

1. Hillel Halkin, "The Oslo Syndrome by Kenneth Levin," *Commentary*, September 2005.

2. Yehuda Elkana, "In Praise of Forgetting" [in Hebrew], *Haaretz*, March 2, 1988. All Elkana quotes in this chapter are drawn from this piece.

3. Spinoza argues for this systematically, following his geometrical method, in the fourth part of the *Ethics*, "Of Human Bondage, or the Power of the Affects." Benedictus de Spinoza, *The Collected Writ-*

ings of Spinoza, 2 vols., ed. and trans. E. Curley (Princeton: Princeton University Press, vol. 1: 1985; vol. 2: 2016).

4. Friedrich Nietzsche, "Twilight of the Idols," in *Nietzsche: The Anti-Christ, Ecce Homo, Twilight of the Idols, and Other Writings*, ed. Aaron Ridley and Judith Norman, trans. Judith Norman (Cambridge: Cambridge University Press, 2005), 159.

5. These and preceding quotes from Nietzsche, "Speech on Redemption," in *Thus Spoke Zarathustra*, eds. Adrian Del Caro and Robert Pippin, trans. Adrian Del Caro (Cambridge: Cambridge University Press, 2006), 111. Translation slightly modified.

6. This pronouncement gave the cue also to Avraham Burg's *The Holocaust is Over; We Must Rise from its Ashes* (or *Defeating Hitler*, as the book was called in Hebrew), trans. Israel Amrani (New York: St. Martin's Press, 2008).

7. Elie Wiesel, *Night*, trans. Marion Wiesel (New York: Hill and Wang, 2006), 64, 63.

8. Wiesel, 64–65.

9. Genesis 22:12 (New King James Version).

10. See also Bernard Avishai's beautiful account of the binding of Isaac's relation to this story in his *New Yorker* obituary of Wiesel: "Postscript: Elie Wiesel, 1928–2016," July 4, 2016.

11. François Mauriac, "Foreword," in Wiesel, *Night*, xxi.

12. Wiesel, "The Nobel Peace Prize Acceptance Speech," in *Night: Memorial Edition* (New York: Hill and Wang, 2017), 133–36.

13. Wiesel, *And the Sea is Never Full: Memoirs, 1969–*, trans. Marion Wiesel (New York: Schocken Books, 1999), 125.

14. Wiesel, *Against Silence*, ed. Irving Abrahamson (New York: Schocken Books, 1984), i, 158, 211.

15. Barack Obama, "Memorial Tribute," in Wiesel, *Night: Memorial Edition*, xi.

16. See Jean Améry, *At the Mind's Limits: Contemplations by a Survivor on Auschwitz and Its Realities* (Bloomington: Indiana University Press, 1980).

17. Primo Levi, *The Reawakening* (New York: Touchstone, 1995), 16.

18. Levi, 206.

19. Much can be learnt from the different adjectives used by Elkana and Wiesel to describe human duty to the past. For the one, remembering is a "sacred" duty; for the other, the duty to forget is "political and educational."

20. Matti Friedman, "What Happens When a Holocaust Memorial Plays Host to Autocrats," *The New York Times*, December 8, 2018.

21. "Yad Vashem Ought not Become a Washing Machine for the Extreme Right" [in German], *Süddeutsche Zeitung*, December 12, 2018.

22. Raphael Ahren, "Palestinians Rap Bennett over Alleged 'Kill Arabs' Remarks," *The Times of Israel*, July 31, 2013.

23. Shai Piron, "Selling the House to an Arab and Moving a Grave" [in Hebrew], *Kipa* (blog), August 9, 2002; see also the answer to the follow-up question, in which Piron suggests that the asker do everything he can to sell to a Jew, and, if necessary, rent it to an Arab to avoid selling the property to a non-Jew.

24. Friedman, "What Happens When a Holocaust Museum Plays Host to Autocrats."

25. Nadav Tamir, "Israel Must Prepare for a Change in US Policy Toward Iran," *The Jerusalem Post*, November 14, 2020.

26. David Ben-Gurion, "The Redemption" [in Yiddish], *Der Yiddischer Kampfer*, November 16, 1917. Translation from Idith Zertal, *Israel's*

Holocaust and the Politics of Nationhood, trans. Chaya Galai (Cambridge: Cambridge University Press, 2005), 93.

27. Ruth Firer, *Agents of Zionist Education* [in Hebrew] (Tel Aviv: Hakibbutz Hameuchad, 1985), 70.

28. See Idith Zertal's exhaustive reconstruction in *Israel's Holocaust and the Politics of Nationhood*, 93–94.

29. Susan Sontag, "Reflections on the Deputy," in *Against Interpretation* (New York: Picador, 2001), 124–31.

30. Ben-Gurion, "Interview with Prime Minister David Ben-Gurion" [in Hebrew], *Yedioth Ahronoth*, March 31, 1961.

31. See Ross Poole's discussion, "Patriotism and Nationalism," in I. Primoraz and A. Paklovic, eds., *Patriotism: Philosophical and Political Perspectives* (Abingdon: Routledge, 2016), 129–46.

32. See, for example, the report on the speech in *The Guardian*: Peter Beaumont, "Anger at Netanyahu Claim Palestinian Grand Mufti Inspired Holocaust," October 21, 2015.

33. Israel Gutman, ed., *The Encyclopedia of the Holocaust* [in Hebrew] (Jerusalem: Yad Vashem Publishing and Sifriyat Poalim, 1990), 4 vols. Interestingly, in the encyclopedia's English version, the ratios are more reasonable.

34. Barak Ravid, "After Labeling Them 'Worse Than Kapos,' U.S. Ambassador to Israel David Friedman Meets with J Street," *Haaretz*, July 3, 2017.

35. For the relation between Holocaust commemoration, Israeli nationhood, and ultimately Rabin's assassination, see Zertal, *Israel's Holocaust and the Politics of Nationhood*, 197–208.

36. Yosef Hayim Yerushalmi, *Zakhor: Jewish Memory and Jewish History* (Seattle: University of Washington Press, 1982), 117.

37. "Ahmad Tibi's Knesset Speech on Holocaust Memorial Day," Jews for Justice for Palestinians (website), January 29, 2010. Translation slightly modified.

CHAPTER 3
REMEMBERING AND FORGETTING: THE NAKBA

1. Hannah Arendt, "Zionism Reconsidered," in *Hannah Arendt, The Jewish Writings*, eds. Jerome Kohn and Ron H. Feldman (New York: Schocken Books, 2007), 343. Unless otherwise noted, Arendt quotes are from this essay. Albert Einstein, who had been invited to become Israel's first president, cosigned a letter drafted by Arendt denouncing Menachem Begin for his fascist record. The open letter, alerting American Jews to the violent methods of Begin's party, Heirut (Liberty), was printed by *The New York Times* on December 4, 1948.

2. Theodor Herzl, *The Complete Diaries of Theodor Herzl*, vol. 1, ed. Raphael Patai, trans. Harry Zohn (New York: Herzl Press, 1960), 88–89.

3. Israel Zangwill, "The Return to Palestine," *New Liberal Review* 2, no. 11 (December 1901): 615.

4. Zangwill, *Speeches, Articles and Letters* (London: The Soncino Press, 1937), 210.

5. Vladimir Jabotinsky, "A Talk with Zangwill," *Jewish Herald*, August 4, 1939.

6. Shabtai Teveth, *Ben-Gurion and the Palestinian Arabs: From Peace to War* (Oxford: Oxford University Press, 1985), 43.

7. David Ben-Gurion, July 12, 1937, diary entry, Ben-Gurion Archives,

Ben-Gurion University of the Negev, Beersheba, Israel. Translation from Benny Morris, *The Birth of the Palestinian Refugee Problem Revisited* (Cambridge: Cambridge University Press, 2004), 46–47.

8. Ben-Gurion, The Twentieth Zionist Congress, Fifth Meeting, Zurich, August 21–23, 1937. Quoted in Benny Morris, *Jews and Arabs in Palestine/Israel, 1936-1956* [in Hebrew] (Tel Aviv: Am Oved, 2004), 46–47.

9. Proceedings of the Board of the Jewish Agency [in Hebrew], May 7, 1944, S100/42b, Central Zionist Archive, Jerusalem.

10. Proceedings of the Board of the Jewish Agency, May 7, 1944.

11. Ben-Gurion, June 12, 1938, diary entry, Ben-Gurion Archives.

12. S. Avigor, B. Dinor, Y. Slotzki, et al., eds., *The Book of the Haganah's Chronicles*, vol. 3 [in Hebrew] (Tel Aviv: Am Oved, 1976), 1955–59.

13. See Morris's account of the event in *The Birth of the Palestinian Refugee Problem Revisited*, 237.

14. Tom Segev, *A State at Any Cost: The Life of David Ben-Gurion* [in Hebrew] (Ben Shemen: Keter, 2018), 400.

15. Morris, *Palestinian Refugee Problem*, 276.

16. Zadok Eshel, *Haganah Battles in Haifa* [in Hebrew] (Tel Aviv: Maarachot, 1978), 356.

17. Eshel, 365. According to Ehud Almog, who was interviewed by *Haaretz*, Davidka shells were used, not three-inch mortars. Otherwise, the description is "correct. Absolutely true." Shay Fogelman, "Port in a Storm," *Haaretz*, June 3, 2011.

18. Morris includes in his Hebrew *Birth of the Palestinian Refugee Problem* only a part of Eshel's quote, omitting the fact that the crowd's shelling was decided once the Haganah had learned that Arabs were

evacuating. Backed by the partial quote, he writes that there's "no evidence" that they thought their actions "would lead to the Arabs' evacuation from Haifa," 123.

19. Public Record Office, wo261-297, "Sitrep No. 10," First Battalion Coldstream Guards, 16:30 hours, April 22, 1948.

20. Golda Meirson, Proceedings of the Board of the Jewish Agency [in Hebrew], May 6, 1948, 45/2, Central Zionist Archive.

21. Yigal Allon and Yitzhak Rabin to the Yiftach and the Eighth Brigades, July 12, 1948, "Lod and Ramleh," Ben-Gurion Archives.

22. Yosef Nahmani, November 6, 1948, diary entry [in Hebrew]. Quoted in Morris, *A Correction of an Error: Arabs and Jews in Eretz Israel, 1936– 1956* [in Hebrew] (Tel Aviv: Am Oved, 2000), 131–32.

23. Morris, *Palestinian Refugee Problem*, 136–37.

24. Yosef Weitz, December 2, 1940, diary entry, in *My Diary and Letters to the Children*, vol. 2 [in Hebrew] (Tel Aviv: Masada, 1965), 181.

25. Quoted in Adam Raz, *Kafr Qasim Massacre* [in Hebrew] (Jerusalem: Carmel, 2018), 42–43.

26. The government's ongoing systematic censorship of documents attesting to the Nakba is familiar. For a recent account, see the research of Akevot, Institute for Israeli-Palestinian Conflict Research, "Silencing: Director of Security of the Defense Establishment's Covering of Archival Documents," July 2019.

27. Rafi Mann, "Talking Values with the Old Man," *Haaretz*, October 29, 2010. All quotes from Oz's meetings with Ben-Gurion are drawn from this article.

28. Avraham Shapira, ed., *Warriors' Conversations* (Tel Aviv: Dfus Ahdut, 1967).

29. Segev, *1967: Israel, The War, and The Year that Transformed the Middle East* (New York: Metropolitan Books, 2007), 443. The above discussion is indebted to Segev, 442–54.

30. Mor Loushy, *Censored Voices* (2015; Chicago, IL: Music Box Films, 2016).

31. Segev, *1967*, 444–46.

32. Ari Shavit, *My Promised Land: The Triumph and Tragedy of Israel* (New York: Spiegel & Grau, 2013).

33. Ari Shavit, "Lydda, 1948: a City, a Massacre and the Middle East Today," *The New Yorker*, October 14, 2013; Thomas Friedman, "Something for Barack and Bibi to Talk About," *The New York Times*, November 16, 2013; Leon Wieseltier, "The State of Israel," *The New York Times*, November 21, 2013; Dwight Garner, "Son of Israel, Caught in the Middle," *The New York Times*, November 19, 2013.

34. Shavit, *My Promised Land*, 398.

35. Shavit, 331.

36. Shavit, 333.

37. Shavit, 108.

38. Shavit, 131.

39. Shavit, 131.

40. Susie Linfield, "Ari Shavit: From Left Field," *Guernica*, December 16, 2013.

41. Barak Ravid, "Lieberman's 'Peace' Plan: Paid Transfer to Israel's Arabs" [in Hebrew], *Haaretz*, November 28, 2014.

42. Yotam Berger, "The National Union Committee Affirmed Plan Calling for the Palestinians' Transfer" [in Hebrew], *Haaretz*, September 13, 2017.

43. Tomer Persico, "Why Religious Zionism is Growing Darker," *Haaretz*, May 16, 2017.

44. Yotam Berger, "The Denied Transfer of the Jewish Home" [in Hebrew], *Haaretz*, September 13, 2017.

45. Ben-Zion Netanyahu, ed., *The Road to Independence: Speeches, Articles, Correspondence* [in Hebrew] (Tel Aviv: Hotza'a Medinit, 1938), xxxvii–xliv.

46. Shabtai Teveth, *The Evolution of "Transfer" in Zionist Thinking* [in Hebrew] (Tel Aviv: Shiloah Institute, 1989), 17.

47. Ari Shavit, "Survival of the Fittest," *Haaretz*, January 8, 2004.

48. Quoted in Yishai Menuchin, ed., *On Democracy and Disobedience* [in Hebrew] (Jerusalem: Yesh Gvul, 1990), 140.

49. Emile Habibi, "Your Holocaust, Our Catastrophe" [in Hebrew], *Politica* 8 (1986): 26.

CHAPTER 4
THE HAIFA REPUBLIC

1. Rick Gladstone and Jodi Rudoren (quoting Nathan Thrall), "Mahmoud Abbas, at U.N., Says Palestinians Are No Longer Bound by Oslo Accords," *The New York Times*, October 1, 2015.

2. Barak Ravid, "Was It a Bombshell or Stink Bomb That Abbas Dropped in His UN Speech?," *Haaretz*, September 30, 2015.

3. Madeline Conway, "Trump Says He Can 'Live With' Either Two-State or One-State Solution for Israel," *Politico*, February 15, 2017.

4. The scene can be watched at ABC News, "Trump, Netanyahu Full Press Conference | ABC News," YouTube, February 15, 2017, https://www.youtube.com/watch?v=SmfseeZt5fA.

5. Stephen Farrell, "Why Is the U.S. Moving Its Embassy to Jerusalem?," Reuters, May 7, 2018.

6. This was Sari Nusseibeh's position. He had been a one-state proponent all along, but became an Arafat advisor and Oslo proponent. See his *Once Upon a Country* (London: Picador, 2008), 364–82.

7. See Peace Now's Settlement Watch at https://peacenow.org.il/settlements-watch/matzav/population, and Shaul Arieli's *Messianism Meets Reality: Vision of Illusion, 1967–2016* [in English] (Tel Aviv: Economic Cooperation Foundation, 2017), both drawing on the Israel Bureau of Statistics.

8. See the official governmental website GovMap.gov.il.

9. GovMap.gov.il. Once one understands the repression of the Nakba's history, it is hard not to see the omitting of Palestinian cities from the map as symbolic of a horrifying future. The Palestinians are, for Israeli students, already not there.

10. Benjamin Netanyahu, "Address by PM Netanyahu at Bar-Ilan University," Israel Ministry of Foreign Affairs (website), June 14, 2009.

11. Jonathan Freedland, "Heroes of 2014: Reuven 'Ruvi' Rivlin, President of Israel," *The Guardian*, December 31, 2014.

12. "177. Memorandum of Conversation, Washington, December 16, 1977, 9–10 a.m.," *Foreign Relations of the United States, 1977–1980*, vol. VIII, Arab-Israeli Dispute, January 1977–August 1978, United States Department of State Office of the Historian (website).

13. Nathan Thrall, *The Only Language They Understand: Forcing Compromise in Israel and Palestine* (New York: Metropolitan Books, 2017), 23.

14. Seth Anziska, *Preventing Palestine: A Political History from Camp David to Oslo* (Princeton: Princeton University Press, 2018).

15. Anziska, 13.

16. "103 Statement to the Knesset by Prime Minister Begin, Presenting Israel's Peace Plan, 28 December 1977," Israel Ministry of Foreign Affairs (website).

17. "103 Statement to the Knesset."

18. Anziska, *Preventing Palestine*, 110.

19. "103 Statement to the Knesset."

20. "103 Statement to the Knesset."

21. David Ben-Gurion, "National Autonomy and Neighbors' Relations," in *Us and Our Neighbors* [in Hebrew] (Tel Aviv: Am Oved, 1931), 111–14, 122–23.

22. Lee Yaron and Josh Breiner, "Thousands Protest Israeli Annexation in Tel Aviv; Bernie Sanders Calls to 'Stand Up to Authoritarian Leaders,'" *Haaretz*, June 6, 2020.

23. Yaron and Breiner, "Thousands Protest Israeli Annexation."

24. Aluf Benn, "The Left's Messianic Stage" [in Hebrew], *Haaretz*, February 5, 2020.

25. Dmitry Shumsky, "A Vote for the Joint List is a Vote for the Two-State Solution" [in Hebrew], *Haaretz*, February 15, 2020. As a side note, it is remarkable that Shumsky, who has done perhaps more than any other expert to bring out the difference between sovereignty and self-determination in Zionism's origins, still supports Jewish sovereignty and the two-state solution.

26. "Odeh: The Joint List Consists in About 90% Arabs, and That's a Disadvantage" (report on the paper's Democracy Conference) [in Hebrew], *Haaretz*, April 5, 2020.

Acknowledgments

As will be apparent to any reader, my thinking on Israel is indebted to the works of Tom Segev, Benny Morris, Dmitry Shumsky, and Idith Zertal. I do not know any of them personally, and do not agree with everything that they wrote, but have attempted to draw on their work—and, naturally, on that of many others—to construct an imaginative political argument that goes beyond their state-of-the-art historical writings. In so doing, I benefited from comments and criticisms provided in numerous conversations with experts, mentors, and friends, including Ross Poole, Yoni Lebowitsch, Susan Neiman, Susie Linfield, Raef Zreik, Philipp Nielsen, Andrew Arato, Itamar Mann, Paul Kottman, Cinzia Arruzza, Sarah Schweig, Roberto Palomba, Jordi Grau-pera, Thomas Meyer, Rebecca Vilkomerson, Jay Bernstein, Richard Bernstein, Thomas Cantone, and Dan Landau. Some of the ideas printed in the following chapters were initially elaborated (and, to a lesser extent, printed) in journalistic pieces, in *The New*

York Times, *Die Zeit*, *Los Angeles Review of Books*, and *Boston Review*. The exchange with some of these paper's editors, especially Adam Soboczynski and Peter Catapano, made a significant impact on my writing, as did Edwin Frank's extensive revisions of the manuscript for New York Review Books. Amanda Gersten improved the text greatly by providing it a final editing.

The time dedicated to finishing this book was enabled by two institutions, the New School for Social Research, which provided a research leave; and the Humboldt Foundation, which supported my stay in Germany. I also benefited from two memorable writing retreats at the Zumthor Ferienhäuser in Leis, Switzerland. Special thanks are due to Jack Miles, for encouraging me to write this book in the first place and then advising more or less on every turn of its argument; to my parents, Eti and Amnon Boehm, for intense support (and also criticism); and to Inbal Hever, for reading and commenting on every word. Thinking about Israel's present and future has become, for better or worse, an indispensable part of our life together. It is to her that this work is dedicated.

OMRI BOEHM
Tel Aviv
April 2021

OMRI BOEHM is an associate professor of philosophy at the New School for Social Research in New York City. He is the author of *The Binding of Isaac: A Religious Model of Disobedience* and *Kant's Critique of Spinoza*. His writings on Israeli politics and culture have appeared in *The New York Times*, *Die Zeit*, and *Haaretz*, among others.